W9-CZT-374

THE SACRED LITERATURE SERIES

Edited by Kerry Brown and Sima Sharma

LAO-TZU'S TREATISE ON THE RESPONSE OF THE TAO

T'AI-SHANG KAN-YING P'IEN

Lao-tzu's Treatise on
The Response of the Tao

Li Ying-chang

Translated with an introduction by Eva Wong

With an historical introduction by Sean Dennison

UNDER THE AUSPICES OF FUNG LOY KOK INSTITUTE OF TAOISM

HarperCollins*Publishers*

For more information about the
International Sacred Literature Trust,
please write to the ISLT at:
23 Darley Avenue, Manchester M20 8ZD
Great Britain

HarperCollins Publishers
1160 Battery Street, San Francisco, CA 94111
United States of America
77–85 Fulham Palace Road, London W6 8JB
Great Britain
25 Ryde Road, Pymble, NSW 2073
Australia

Designed by Caro Inglis
Proofread by Anne Hegerty
Photoset in Linotron Sabon by Northern
Phototypsetting Company Limited,
Bolton, U. K.

Library of Congress Cataloging-in-Publication Data
T'ai-shang kan-ying p'ien. English.
Lao-tzu's treatise on the response of the Tao : T'ai-shang kan-ying p'ien / Li
Ying-chang ; translated with an introduction by Eva Wong. — 1st ed.
p. cm.
Includes bibliographical references.
ISBN 0–06–064956–9 (alk. paper)
1. Conduct of life—Early works to 1800. 2. Taoism. I. Li, Ying-chang,
12th cent. II. Wong, Eva. III. Title.
BJ1558.C5T313 1994
299'.51444—dc20   93–49773
                                                   CIP

94 95 96 97 98 CWI 10 9 8 7 6 5 4 3 2 1

This edition is printed on acid-free paper that meets the American
National Standards Institute Z39.48 Standard.

*To Master Moy Lin-shin, who made the Taoist teachings available
to me and all those who wish to learn*

The International Sacred Literature Trust was established to promote understanding and open discussion between and within faiths and to give voice in today's world to the wisdom that speaks across time and traditions.

What resources do the sacred traditions of the world possess to respond to the great global threats of poverty, war, ecological disaster and spiritual despair?

Our starting-point is the sacred texts with their vision of a higher truth and their deep insights into the nature of humanity and the universe we inhabit. The translation programme is planned so that each faith community articulates its own teachings with the intention of enhancing its self-understanding as well as the understanding of those of other faiths and those of no faith.

The Trust particularly encourages faiths to make available texts which are needed in translation for their own communities and also texts which are little known outside the tradition but which have the power to inspire, console, enlighten and transform. These sources from the past become resources for the present and future when we make inspired use of them to guide us in shaping the contemporary world.

Our religious traditions are diverse but, as with the natural environment, we are discovering the global interdependence of human hearts and minds. The Trust invites all to participate in the modern experience of interfaith encounter and exchange which marks a new phase in the human quest to discover our full humanity.

Contents

List of Illustrations xi

Acknowledgments xiii

Historical Introduction xv

Translator's Introduction xxvii

Dates of the Chinese Dynasties xxxxiv

LAO-TZU'S TREATISE ON
THE RESPONSE OF THE TAO

1. Understanding the Principles 3

2. Words of Warning 5

3. The Guardians 9

4. Accumulating Good Works 13

5. Reward for Good Deeds 17

6. Evil Deeds 19

7. Retribution for Evil Deeds 25

8. Instructions on Important Principles 29

9. Repentance 31

10. Actions 33

FOLK TALES

The Light of Truth 37

The Pious Scholar's Fortune 41

Charity Rewarded 45

CONTENTS

The Power of a Good Person's Name   49

A Bully's Reform   53

The Irresponsible Minister   57

A Visit to Hell   61

Disrespect for Sacred Texts   65

Punishment Apportioned to Crime   69

The North Star Constellation   73

Offence against a Deity   77

The God of the Hearth   81

The Dragon Lord's Wrath   89

Ho-kuan and the Ants   93

The Cruel Hunters   97

Fung Loy Kok Institute of Taoism   101

List of Illustrations

WOODCUTS

1. Lao-tzu   35

2. Wan Teh-hsu is received by the Lords of Heaven   36

3. The pious scholar Shang Shih-ying is introduced to the
   Emperor   40

4. The benevolent governor is attended by immortals   44

5. The bully is reprimanded by the old gentleman   52

6. Minister Wang An-shih is tortured in Hell   56

7. Ch'uan Ju-yu visits Hell   60

8. P'ang Heng-hsiu prostrates himself before the deities of the
   North Star Constellation   72

9. The Goddess of the Water Realm punishes the student   76

10. The Dragon Lord sends a storm   88

11. Ho-kuan visits the kingdom of the ants   92

12. The cruel hunters shoot at the deer spirit   96

PLATE

Master Moy Lin-shin   *Facing page* 101

Acknowledgments

I would like to thank the members of the Fung Loy Kok Translation Committee – Sean Dennison, Philippe Gagnon, Karen Laughlin and Jim Nicholson – for reviewing the earlier drafts of the manuscripts. Also, many thanks to the friends and members of the Fung Loy Kok Institute of Taoism for supporting the translation project. Finally, I am indebted to my teacher, Master Moy Lin-shin, for giving me the teachings of Taoism.

Eva Wong

We acknowledge and thank:

Quentin Smith, L. K. Sharma, Doreen Mantle and Shashwati Sharma for their ideas and constant support; Josephine Edwards for her diligence and helpfulness in administering the Trust; Oliver Caldecott, Mark Cohen, Ivan Hattingh, Jack Hogbin, Martin Palmer, Aubrey Rose and the International Consultancy on Religion, Education and Culture for their time and commitment in the founding years of the ISLT; Professor T. H. Barrett, Chair of East Asian History in the School of Oriental and African Studies at London University, for the time and trouble he has taken to advise and guide the ISLT in developing its Taoist series.

International Sacred Literature Trust

Historical Introduction

At dawn in Hong Kong, Beijing, London, Paris, New York, or Sydney, indeed in almost any major city, there are people in the parks performing a very graceful, slow-motion exercise called *T'ai Chi Ch'uan* (Grand Ultimate Movements). Though there are both lay and monastic transmissions of this Taoist art, it is for many their first encounter with Taoism as a living tradition. It certainly was for me, but that was nearly twenty years ago. Now, as a Westerner dedicated to Taoist training, I have learned that understanding comes only through practice, and the aim of Taoist practice is to return to the Tao, the source of all life, through the cultivation of mind and body.

Taoism is a rich and dynamic tradition which has continued to develop for over four thousand years. Through the centuries, Taoism has evolved in both theory and practice. It is said that people make Taoism, as Taoism guides people's actions. It is not a static religion, but a flexible and dynamic one, adapting to the times and to prevailing social conditions.

Taoism's roots reach back to the shamanistic songs and dances of ancient China, which contributed images and ritual practices to later Taoist liturgies and ceremonies and gave early Taoists models of techniques of longevity. But the origin of Taoism as a philosophy is often traced to Lao-tzu, generally thought to have been born in 571 BCE. Lao-tzu lived during a period when China was in a state of civil war. In a time of suffering and conflict, he advocated peaceful and harmonious coexistence, simplicity of living, appreciation of the natural way of things, and the value of life. In the *Tao-te Ching*, Lao-tzu taught that the Tao is the origin of the universe and the source of life. All existence derives from the Tao, the undifferentiated, complete reality that existed before Heaven and Earth. It is the life force of all things, animate and inanimate. When nature and humanity follow the way of the Tao, they are filled with the life force. When they depart from the Tao, they gradually decay and die. The Tao is also the goal of human life, which is itself a path of return: "When your constant virtue does not go astray, you'll return to the condition which has no limit (*wu-chi*)."[1]

Lao-tzu taught that there is a spark of goodness within each of us.

This is the original nature with which we are born. As we interact with the world around us, our original nature becomes clouded; we become self-centred and accumulate vices, desires and anxieties. Through inner stillness and control of our breath we seek to eliminate these weaknesses so that our original nature can again shine brightly, guiding our thoughts and actions. Later, this was called "cultivation of original mind".

Lao-tzu also advocated cultivation of the health of the body or returning to what is known as the "original body". This body is not only flexible and full of vitality but is also, like that of the ancient shamans, resistant to illness and injury: "One who embraces the fullness of virtue can be compared to a newborn babe. Wasps and scorpions, snakes and vipers do not sting him; birds of prey and fierce beasts do not seize him."[2]

Taoism is perhaps unique among philosophies because of its equal emphasis on cultivating both mind and body. The theory of cultivating the body was developed through a long history of interaction between Taoism and Chinese medicine. Fundamental to Taoism is the idea that health involves balance and circulation of energy in the body. We are endowed with this energy at birth but bad habits, poor posture, negative attitudes and unhealthy lifestyles dissipate the energy. This causes weak health and decreased immunity to disease and illness. Taoist sages from the time of Lao-tzu have researched and developed methods of regaining lost health and improving the quality of life through exercises, meditation and a simple lifestyle.

Chuang-tzu, a second major figure in the history of Taoism, lived approximately four hundred years after Lao-tzu in the second century BCE. The texts attributed to Chuang-tzu relate shamanistic practices more specifically to the characteristically Taoist emphasis on the cultivation of body and mind as parallel but not yet synthesized training. He developed two models of enlightenment, one a contemplative inner stillness, the other an ecstatic, mystical state that made the "ideal being" impervious to illness or harm. Yet the seed of relating these two models was already present in his discussion of meditation techniques and deep breathing: "Enfold the spirit in quietude and the body will right itself . . . when the eye does not see, the ear does not hear, and the mind does not know, then your spirit will protect the body, and the body will enjoy long life."[3]

For Chuang-tzu, there is an analogy between the internal universe and external universe, between the human body and the world. Inside the body are mountains, valleys, rivers and streams. Energy circulates in this internal universe as it does in nature. At death, this energy is released and returned to its source. The being that Chuang-tzu calls the "True Man" does not fear death because he returns the energy as he received it, pure and uncontaminated by desires or anxieties: "The True Man did not forget where he began; he did not try to find out where he would end. He received something and took pleasure in it; he forgot about it and handed it back again."[4]

The interrelationship of mind and body and of the inner and outer world is deepened in Chuang-tzu's teaching that extreme emotions damage health and attachment to sensations brings harm, not just to the individual but to the community.

> Are men exceedingly joyful? They will do damage to the yang element. Are men exceedingly angry? They will do damage to the yin. And when both yin and yang are damaged, the four seasons will not come as they should, heat and cold will fail to achieve their proper harmony, and this in turn will do harm to the bodies of men . . . Then for the first time the world grows restless and aspiring.
>
> Do men delight in what they see? They are corrupted by colours. Do they delight in what they hear? They are corrupted by sounds . . . if the world does not rest in the true form of its nature and fate, then the eight delights will begin to grow warped and crooked, jumbled and deranged, and will bring confusion to the world.[5]

But it was Chang Tao-liang, patriarch of the Lunghushan Sect of Taoism, who transformed Taoist philosophy into a formal religion in the second century, choosing Lao-tzu as its patriarch and establishing ceremonies, a hierarchy of priests, and an early form of monastic life.

Lao-tzu was now held as a manifestation of the Tao and appeared in many forms, including that of the Three Pure Ones: the Lord of Wu-chi (the condition without limit), the Lord of the Precious Spirit and the Lord of Virtue. The Lord of Wu-chi resides in the Jade Pure Realm, which is the highest realm where the Way of Heaven dominates and things have not separated from the Tao. The Lord of the

Precious Spirit resides in the Most Pure Realm, which is the middle realm where the Way of the Earth dominates and yin and yang have merged but are still rooted in the underlying unity of wu-chi. The Lord of Virtue resides in the High Pure Realm, which is the lower realm where the Way of Humanity dominates and differentiation has created the "ten thousand myriad things" of existence.

Philosophical Taoism continued to evolve into a sophisticated system, with a distinct cosmology and set of spiritual practices. Chu-hsi of the Sung dynasty (960–1279 CE) further developed the Taoist understanding of the origin of the universe and life. He described it as an ongoing process of differentiation, beginning from the Tao or wu-chi and proceeding through the interaction of the complementary forces of yin and yang:

> From wu-chi comes t'ai-chi. When t'ai-chi moves, it creates yang. When movement reaches its extreme, stillness emerges. In stillness, yin is born. Thus, movement and stillness follow each other. Yin and yang, movement and stillness, form the force of creation. From yang and yin are created the elements water, fire, wood, metal and earth. The five vapours mutually enrich each other and generate the four seasons. The five elements originate from yin and yang. Yin and yang originate from t'ai-chi and t'ai-chi originates from wu-chi. From the properties of the five elements and the essence of wu-chi emerges generative energy. From the Way of Heaven, male is born. Following the Way of Earth, female is born. The union of Heaven and Earth gives rise to the ten thousand myriad things. The ten thousand myriad things procreate and contribute to many forms of existence whose origin is wu-chi.[6]

Taoist arts and spiritual practices seek to restore the balance of yin and yang and to reverse this process of differentiation, thereby returning to the wholeness that is the Tao.

The Three Vehicles

The Three Pure Ones came to represent three levels of enlightenment or return to the origin. To attain the High Pure Realm is to exist in harmony with nature and humanity, to live according to the laws of nature, and to embody the highest virtues of humanity. To enter the Most Pure Realm is to exist in a state in which subject and object are differentiated but are integral parts of the Tao. To rise to the Jade Pure Realm is to attain wu-chi, the complete union with the Tao.

Similarly, Taoist training can be divided into three paths called the Lower, Middle and Higher Vehicles. The Lower Vehicle focuses on action and good works in the community. The cultivation of virtue and compassion is the primary goal of training. Advancement along this path is gradual but safe, since this vehicle does not involve methods that change the mind and body through alchemical trans-formations. Practice of the Lower Vehicle does not require monastic transmission. Therefore, this is the easiest path to follow.

The Middle Vehicle is the path of devotion. The cultivation of humility and sacrifice is accomplished through chanting the scriptures and observing the Taoist festivals. Advancement along this path is faster, but practice of this vehicle requires the support of a temple-based community since ceremonial and liturgical practices are available only within a temple setting.

The Higher Vehicle is the path of internal alchemy. The cultivation of body and mind is achieved through rigorous techniques of emptying the mind and tempering the body. It is said that enlightenment may be achieved in a single lifetime through this vehicle. However, practice of this vehicle requires guidance from an enlightened teacher, a sup-portive community, and the predisposition of the practitioner. The Higher Vehicle is the fastest path to enlightenment, but it is also the most dangerous. An erroneous step will lead to disastrous conse-quences for both physical and mental health.

The Five Schools

Contemporary Taoist sects can be divided into five major schools, each characterized by a particular emphasis in theory and practice. Each school can also be characterized by its affiliation with the Lower, Middle or Higher Vehicle. Some schools focus exclusively on one vehicle of training while others offer all three paths. Sects existing within each school differ in techniques of training but share a similar theoretical orientation. Though Westerners know Taoism primarily through the texts of Lao-tzu and Chuang-tzu, the teachings of the five schools are incorporated in more than 1,600 volumes of the Taoist canon, which developed over the centuries and remains the primary source of knowledge about Taoist beliefs and practices.

Action and Karma School

Focusing on the Lower Vehicle, the school of Action and Karma Taoism advocates charitable works and sacrifice of self to help others. Good deeds sow the fruit of good karma. With the accumulation of good works, liberation from suffering and reincarnation can be achieved. The emphasis on action and karma is reflected in the focus on confession, retribution, and reward in their scriptures, particularly in the stories of *Lao-tzu's Treatise on the Response of the Tao (T'ai-shang Kan-ying P'ien)*.

One representative sect of this school is the Lushan sect, which dates from the Southern Sung dynasty (1127–1279 CE) and shows a strong influence from Mahayana Buddhism. The sect achieved its height of development during the Ming dynasty (1368–1644 CE). Because the transmission of its teachings does not require a monastic environment, this school has attracted many lay practitioners. This sect is known for its emphasis on lay practice and social ethics since virtue and charity can be cultivated outside a monastic setting. Moreover, Lushan has retained a close relationship with the Mahayana Buddhists, acknowledging Buddha as a Taoist deity and adopting many Buddhist sutras.

Ceremonial School

Ceremonial Taoism exemplifies the Middle Vehicle, advocating the purification and cultivation of self through ceremonies and chanting of the scriptures. Through devotion and confession, the union of humanity and the Tao is achieved. Two scriptures often chanted in Taoist ceremonies are the *North and South Star Liturgies*. The North Star is the ruler of all heavenly bodies. It is said to be the palace of the Jade Emperor, a Taoist deity who is the keeper of virtue and who holds authority over health and longevity. If the North Star or Jade Emperor is the guide of our actions, then virtue will direct us and we will lead a long and healthy life. The North Star is a stable star, while all other stars revolve around it. The North Star therefore represents the underlying reality of the Tao, that aspect of the Tao which is eternal and unchanging. The moving stars, including the South Star, are fluctuations of the Tao, the appearances which change with space and time.

Both the Laofoushan sect and the Lunghushan (Dragon-tiger) sect represent the Ceremonial School. The Lunghushan sect dates from the Eastern Han period (25–220 CE), but its emphasis on ceremonies did not emerge until Tao Kuang-t'ing collected and compiled the ceremonial liturgies of Taoism. The Laofoushan sect was an off-shoot of the Lunghushan sect. The Laofoushan sect does not acknowledge Chang Tao-liang, the Heavenly Teacher of the Lunghushan sect, as its patriarch. Its liturgy therefore omitted sections of the Lunghushan liturgy that placed Chang as the next highest deity under Lao-tzu. The Laofoushan sect originated in the Sui dynasty (589–618 CE) but did not become prominent until the Southern Sung.

Internal Alchemical School

Internal Alchemical Taoism typifies the Higher Vehicle. In China, as in the West, alchemy was often understood in material terms, as the transformation of base metals into gold. Taoist internal alchemy seeks to give its practitioners the benefits of mental and physical health and longevity rather than the more transient benefit of material wealth. The alchemical or transformation process therefore involves transforming both body and mind to higher levels of functioning. Central to the transformation process is work with three energies, also known as the Three Treasures (generative, vital and spirit energies). Gathering, purifying, and circulating the Three Treasures leads to the emergence of the spirit-god *(yuan-shen)* and the return to the Tao. Body and mind come together in the crucible of Taoist internal alchemy. One cannot transform the body without the mind and vice versa.

The alchemical work is described in many Taoist texts, among them *Cultivating Stillness* and *Understanding Reality*. But virtually all of these texts emphasize the fact that the practices they describe are part of an oral tradition. According to *Cultivating Stillness*, "the person who does not receive instructions from an enlightened teacher but only looks for the Tao in books, does not recognize the Tao as supreme and precious."[7]

Internal alchemical sects include the Lungmen (Dragon-gate) sect, representing the Northern branch of Complete Reality Taoism, the Tzu-yang sect, representing the Southern branch of Complete Reality Taoism, the Huashan sect and its branch the Hsien T'ien Wu-chi sect, and the Wu-tang Shan sect.

The Complete Reality School was founded by Shao-yang Tzu. His teachings were transmitted to Chung Li-ch'uan and thereafter passed on to Lü Tung-pin. Lü Tung-pin's disciples were Wang Chung-yang and Liu Hai-ch'an. During the Southern Sung dynasty, Wang Chung-yang's disciple, Chiu Ch'ang-ch'un, founded the Lungmen sect and started the Northern branch of Complete Reality Taoism. Liu Hai-ch'an transmitted the teachings to Chang Po-tuan (also known as Chang Tzu-yang). Chang Tzu-yang founded the Tzu-yang sect and started the Southern branch of Complete Reality Taoism. The Northern branch taught "singular" or celibate methods while the Southern branch included both celibate and sexual yogic techniques.

The Huashan sect originated as the Wen-shih sect. The founder, Kuan Wen-shih, was reputed to have lived in the latter part of the Warring States Period (475–221 BCE). During the T'ang dynasty (618–906 CE), the teachings of Wen-shih were transmitted to Mah-I, who in turn taught Chen Hsi-I, the Grand Patriarch of Huashan. According to Sung dynasty chronicles, Chen Hsi-I, who lived in the period of transition from the T'ang to the Northern Sung, also received teachings from Lü Tung-pin. Chen Hsi-I invented the *Liu He Pa Fa*, a system of internal martial arts, to complement the non-non-moving meditative techniques of Complete Reality Taoism. From Mah-I he acquired an understanding of the *I Ching*. Using knowledge from many streams of Taoism, Chen Hsi-I originated a system of internal alchemy that combined moving and non-moving meditation, and the postures of *chi-kung* (the art of circulating internal energy). Chen Hsi-I was famous for his sleeping chi-kung, and for his theory of internal changes based on an understanding of the *I Ching*.

The Huashan lineage branched to form the Hsien T'ien Wu-ch'i

(Earlier Heaven Condition without Limit) sect during the time of Patriarch T'ien-lung in the latter part of the Southern Sung dynasty. Fung Loy Kok Institute of Taoism traces its lineage through the Hsien T'ien Wu-ch'i sect.

The Wu-tang Shan sect was founded by Chang San-feng, who lived toward the end of the Southern Sung and early Yuan dynasties. Chang San-feng is acknowledged as the originator of T'ai Chi Ch'uan, the system of movement for external tempering and internal transformation of the body that is now becoming well known in the West.

The Talismanic School

The school of Talismanic Taoism emphasizes the opening of channels of communication between humanity and the energies resident in the universe. Using mantras, magic, talismans (scripts of power) and amulets, this school focuses on the cooperation of humanity and the Tao in influencing the destiny of humankind.

The Lunghushan (Dragon-tiger) sect and the Maoshan sect are the principal examples of this school. As previously mentioned, the Lunghushan sect, which also represents Ceremonial Taoism, was founded by the descendants of Chang Tao-liang of the Eastern Han dynasty. The sect is transmitted through the Chang family and is currently in its sixty-fourth generation of transmission. The current Patriarch of the Lunghushan sect lives in Taiwan. The Maoshan sect was founded during the Chin dynasty (265–420 CE) by three brothers whose family name was Mao. It is a sister-sect of Lunghushan and is characterized by its emphasis on the use of magic and the acquisition of power from external forces such as deities and nature spirits.

These two sects differ primarily in their magic and uses of talismans. The talismans of the Lunghushan sect draw their power from their patriarch, Chang Tao-liang, whom they acknowledge as a powerful immortal. The magical power of the Maoshan sect is obtained through channelling and calling on deities to enter the body of the practitioner. Their talismans invoke mantras, power-diagrams, and names of figures from a wide range of deities in the Taoist pantheon.

Divinational School

The school of Divinational Taoism focuses on the understanding of the forces of heaven, earth, and humanity so as to live in harmony with the Tao and to predict the events of the future. Most sects practice some form of Divinational Taoism. The Maoshan and Lunghushan sects incorporate divination as part of their magical practices.

Divinational Taoism originated with the *fang-shih*, magicians, diviners and mendicant monks, who thrived in Chinese society from the late Warring States Period to the Wei and Chin dynasties. The fang-shih were also adept in the arts of health and longevity. After the Six Dynasties Period (420–589 CE), the fang-shih became synonymous with the *tao-shih* (Taoist monks). *Fang-shu* (the art of the fang-shih) became synonymous with the Taoist arts, which included internal alchemy, divination, magic, and medicine.

It should be noted that many sects embrace the principles of more than one school of Taoist thought, as they seek to follow the ways of nature to return to the Tao. For example, all sects advocate compassion and charitable works. The difference between the Lushan sect of the Action and Karma School and the Lungmen and Huashan sects of the Internal Alchemy School is that while the Lushan sect focuses on the relationship between good works and karma, the Lungmen and Huashan sects see compassion as a way of cultivating an egoless mind.

Of the schools of Taoism, Action and Karma has the most practitioners today. Its lay transmission and its non-esoteric teachings are responsible for its wide appeal. Ceremonial and Talismanic Taoism are represented by the Lunghushan sect and are popular throughout Chinese communities in Asia. This sect has a large following of believers, but only the initiated priests are considered practitioners. Divinational Taoism is practised by both lay and temple communities. The Lungmen sect and the Hsien T'ien Wu-ch'i sect of Internal Alchemy Taoism have maintained an influential temple system, but the art of longevity is known by few even within these sects.

The appeal of Taoism is also very strong in modern Western society. Many people are drawn to Taoist arts such as T'ai Chi Ch'uan as a means of promoting health and inner peace. These arts represent the culmination of centuries of research and development and offer a clear and integrated method of cultivating mind and body. Although it originated thousands of years ago in China, the philosophy of Taoism is very practical and remarkably relevant to modern life and is not bound by any particular culture. In keeping with the Taoist tradition of adaptation to times and conditions, the Taoist arts are currently being enhanced through dialogue with Western medical science. And through the translations made possible through the International Sacred Literature Trust, we look forward to the wisdom of Taoism continuing to be available to future generations.

Sean Dennison

NOTES

1 Lao-tzu, *Tao Te Ching*, trans. Robert G. Henricks (Ballantine Books, New York, 1989), 80.
2 Ibid., 24.
3 Burton Watson (trans.), *The Complete Works of Chuang Tzu* (Columbia University Press, New York, 1968), 119.
4 Ibid., 78.
5 Ibid., 114–115.
6 Chu-hsi, trans. Fung Loy Kok Institute of Taoism (unpublished).
7 Eva Wong (trans.), *Cultivating Stillness* (Shambhala, Boston & London, 1992), 30.

Translator's Introduction

For eight hundred years, the *T'ai-shang Kan-ying P'ien (Lao-tzu's Treatise on the Response of the Tao)* has been one of the most widely-read Taoist scriptures of the Chinese people. Its straight-forward, practical approach to ethics, lack of the complexities found in more esoteric Taoist texts, and entourage of colourful, moral tales, which arose over the centuries to illustrate its teachings, have ensured its lasting popularity. Furthermore, it belongs to the Action and Karma School of Taoism which does not require a temple or monastic environment for the transmission of its teachings. Anyone can read about and practise this form of Taoism without training with a spiritual master. The *T'ai-shang Kan-ying P'ien* offers the reader a moral code, a method of cultivating health and fulfilling spiritual needs while maintaining a conventional social and professional life. So it is hardly surprising that it has attracted both Taoists and non-Taoists and is regarded by many as an essential guide to living.

The *T'ai-shang Kan-ying P'ien* was written by Li Ying-chang, the founder of the Action and Karma School of Taoism (see p. xx), who lived in the twelfth century during the Southern Sung dynasty. Very little is known of Li Ying-chang's life, except that he began his academic career as a Confucian scholar. Attracted by the philosophy of Taoism in later life, he retired from the civil service (in Confucian China, one of the most respected professions) and became a teacher of Taoism.

The school that Li Ying-chang founded with his treatise, and the moral stories that amplified its message, popularized the ancient Chinese idea that Heaven rewards good actions and delivers retribution for bad ones. It also integrated the spiritual and physical world at the most immediate and personal level by associating one's own health and lifespan with the morality of one's actions. With this as its basic philosophy, the Action and Karma School advocates charitable works as the fundamental spiritual practice. Good deeds sow the seeds of good karma, or positive consequences in terms of health, long life, and general material and spiritual well-being. This is the basic teaching of the *T'ai-shang Kan-ying P'ien,* particularly relevant in today's world where health and longevity have become obsessions with no reference to the spiritual and ethical dimension of life.

The book is credited to the great sage who inspired it: "T'ai-shang" means "the Most High" and is a name given to Lao-tzu, the founder of Taoism, who lived over 2,500 years ago in the sixth century BCE; "kan-ying" means "response"; "p'ien" simply means "treatise". Therefore the English translation of the title is *Lao-tzu's Treatise on the Response of the Tao (or Heaven)*.

The treatise and its stories were first translated into English by Christian missionaries and Buddhist scholars (Douglas Legge in 1891; Carus and Suzuki in 1906) who recognized that to understand the morality of the Chinese people they needed to understand this book. Furthermore, much of the ethical teaching in the work is consistent with both Christian and Buddhist morality.

Now, as the interest and appeal of Taoism widens in Western societies, the task of Taoist temple scholars and scribes has gone beyond copying, editing and writing commentaries on Taoist texts for the Chinese population. It has expanded to include translation of the Taoist texts to make the wisdom of Taoism available to practitioners who do not read Chinese as well as to the general public. The present translation, which is of the *T'ai-shang Kan-ying P'ien* and of fifteen stories which illustrate it, seeks to introduce a representative text of Taoism to Western readers through the perspective of those who practise the tradition.

Although the contemporary temple scholars of the Fung Loy Kok Institute of Taoism work in a different social and cultural environment from their predecessors, the work they do is very similar. Preparation of a text for translation involves familiarity, through practice, with the philosophy of the text. Many of the texts of Taoism contain descriptions of spiritual experiences and of techniques for attaining such experiences. They also use terms whose meanings are only transmitted to initiates within the tradition. Thus, to capture the essence of Taoism in a translation, the translator must have practised and be familiar with the spiritual phenomena described in the texts.

The translation of a text is, therefore, the culmination of years of study, beginning with research into the historical and philosophical background. Various copies of the text are checked and differences resolved. The text is often memorized and studied until the contents become lived experience. When the background preparations are completed, an initial translation is made from the memorized text. This allows the translation to have an intuitive feel rather than being a linear transcription of the words. The translated text is then revised with reference to the original work. Comments from other temple scholars are also incorporated at this stage. Next, the text is subjected to literary and stylistic scrutiny to ensure that the language and style are appropriate for the intended readership. Only then is the text released by the Institute for publication.

The Taoist Canon

The Taoist canon of 1,600 texts is derived from the five main schools of Taoism: Action and Karma, Ceremonial (Devotional), Internal Alchemical, Talismanic (or Magical) and Divinational Taoism (for further details about the schools, see pp. xix–xxv). The canon covers virtually all areas of Chinese knowledge and wisdom, including the sciences of medicine, metallurgy, chemistry, geography and astronomy. It encompasses the humanities in works of poetry and moral tales. There are liturgies, treatises on spiritual practices such as ethics, meditation, exercises for internal hygiene and dietary regulations. Metaphysics (cosmology and the theory of human nature), epistemology (the theory of knowledge and the mind) and the practical arts of divination, diplomacy and military strategy all find their place in this great corpus.

The handful of Action and Karma scriptures, with *Lao-tzu's Treatise on the Response of the Tao* as their centrepiece, are only a tiny fraction of the canon, but this does not mean that the teachings of the school are insignificant. On the contrary, compared with the other schools of Taoism, Action and Karma, with its simple, no-nonsense teachings and its emphasis on lay life, has the largest number of followers. The limited number of texts of this school also suggests that there is little disagreement among the practitioners of this school on the interpretation and practice of its teachings.

Background of *Lao-tzu's Treatise on the Response of the Tao*

The Action and Karma School originated as a distinct tradition in the twelfth century during the early Southern Sung dynasty, and reached the height of its development in the Ming dynasty of the late fourteenth to seventeenth centuries. As noted earlier, the teachings of this school of Taoism centre on reward and retribution. This was a key concept in traditional Chinese beliefs even before the emergence of Taoism as a philosophy in the sixth century BCE. Its origins lie in the notion that one brings disaster on oneself and the community if the Will of Heaven is opposed. And, since the Will of Heaven is manifested in harmony, peace and goodness, actions counter to these ideals would invite retribution from Heaven. With Taoism, the Tao or "Way", which is the impersonal Law of the Universe, became equated with the older concept of the Will of Heaven.

Early Taoism

The ideas of reward and retribution are present in early Taoist texts such as *The Classic of Great Peace (T'ai-ping Ching)*, believed to have been written in the first centuries of the common era during the Eastern Han period. Chapter 18, scroll 2 warns: "Accumulate good works, and prosperity will come to you from the Tao." This would be echoed one thousand years later in chapter 5 of *The Response of the Tao*: "Those who are compassionate are respected by all. The Way of Heaven will guide and protect them. Prosperity will follow them."

Nevertheless, early Taoism, as popularly practised, focused either on the internal alchemical practices of cultivating the internal energies of the body and mind or on the devotional-magical practices of ceremony, scriptural chanting and invocation of deities. Wei Po-yang's *Triplex Unity (Tsan-tung-chi)*, also written in the first centuries CE during the Eastern Han dynasty, sparked a major movement in Taoism of practical arts to prolong life. While such internal alchemical practices attracted the emperors, the nobility and the intelligentsia, the peasants continued to be devoted to folk deities whose origins date back to prehistoric China. These folk beliefs were instrumental in the development of the schools of Devotional (Ceremonial) and Talismanic (Magical) Taoism. Because of the intelligentsia's patronage of the Internal Alchemical School and the peasants' loyalty to Devotional and Talismanic Taoism, beliefs in reward and retribution were overshadowed.

In this context, the admonition of *The Jade Seal Classic (Yu-ch'ien Ching)*, another text from the Eastern Han period, was perhaps a voice from the shadows: "Those who wish to attain immortality should practice filial piety, compassion, friendliness and trustworthiness. A person who simply pursues esoteric techniques but does not perform virtuous deeds will never attain immortality. No benefit can be gained from taking herbs or pills before the full quota of merit has been acquired."

This was voiced again by the great Taoist sage Ko-hung who lived in the fourth and early fifth centuries CE during the Eastern Chin dynasty. The works of Ko-hung decisively linked health and lifespan – a preoccupation of all the social classes – with ethical behaviour, and, in doing so, sowed the seeds for *The Response of the Tao* eight centuries later. According to Ko-hung, the arts of health and longevity such as those expounded by Wei Po-yang's *Triplex Unity* were enhanced by living an ethical life. In chapter 6 of his *The Inner Chapters of the Master Who Embraces Simplicity (Pao-p'u-tzu nei-p'ien)*, Ko-hung describes a contented life as the direct consequence of good works:

> Those who wish to live the fullness of life must accumulate good works, be kind to others, practise charity and have compassion on even the creatures that crawl. They must help the poor, harm no living thing, rejoice in the good fortune of others and share in the suffering of others. They must also utter no curses, look on the failure and success of others as their own, harbour no jealousy of their betters and conceal no evil intentions behind good speech. In this way, they embody virtue and receive rewards from heaven.

These ideas are found in a remarkably similar passage in chapter 4 of *The Response of the Tao*:

> If you are in harmony with the Tao you will advance . . . Be kind and compassionate to all things. Be dedicated in whatever you do . . . Help orphans and widows. Respect the old and care for the

young. Do not hurt trees, grass, and insects. Share in the suffering of others. Delight in the joys of others. Help people in desperate need. Save people from harm. View the good fortune of others as your good fortune. View the losses of others as your own loss.

Of retribution, chapter 6 in Ko-hung's classic says:

When you interfere with another person's property, your wife, children and other members of your household may suffer the consequences. Their lives may even be shortened. And if your wrongdoing does not bring death upon your family, they may suffer from floods, fires, burglaries and other disasters. Therefore, the Taoists say that whenever a person has been killed wrongfully, vengeful killings will follow. Wealth acquired through unethical actions will lead to resentment.

Buddhism and Taoism

In the fourth century a group of Buddhist monks from India arrived in China. However, it was not until almost two hundred years later that the Chinese accepted Buddhism and made it a part of their intellectual heritage. During this time, the Buddhist scriptures were translated from Sanskrit into Chinese, and gradually Buddhism shed its Indian image and blended itself into Chinese culture.

Buddhism's formative period in China was in the sixth century when it incorporated Chinese folk beliefs regarding heaven, Hell and a pantheon of deities. In the seventh century, after the Sui dynasty, a popular Buddhism emerged emphasizing devotion to the Buddhist deities and a literal belief in karmic retribution.

The Response of the Tao was written before attempts were made to synthesize Buddhism, Taoism and the social order of Confucianism. It contains no mention of the Buddhist idea of reincarnation, nor are there references to the Buddhist deities. On the contrary, the deities mentioned are Taoist with their origins in the folk religions (see below). However, the Action and Karma School entered another phase of development in the Ming dynasty of the fourteenth to seventeenth centuries. Taoist ideas of reward and retribution became entwined with the Buddhist ideas of karma, reincarnation and punishment in Hell. As we shall see, this evolution of the Action and Karma School is apparent in some of the stories, included in this volume, that grew up around *The Response of the Tao*, probably during the Ming period.

Folk Traditions and Taoism

While the influence of Buddhism on the *The Response of the Tao* is largely to be found in the later stories which accompany it, the influence of the folk religions of China, incorporated into Taoism much earlier, can be seen in the text proper. As with other Taoist scriptures written after the Eastern Han Period, this text contains references to folk deities such as the God of the Hearth, also known as the Kitchen God, Hsi Wang-mu, also known as the Mother Empress of the West, the North Star deities, and Wen-ch'ang Ti-chun, Patron of the Arts and Literature. Whether taken literally or symbolically, all these deities predate the emergence of Taoism as an organized religion. The origin of Wen-ch'ang Ti-chun can be traced back to a thunder god of the Szechuan region popular during the first century CE. The North Star or the Great Bear (Pei-tou Star) was the highest of the nine levels of heaven where the supreme ruler of both heaven and earth lived. Its worship was recorded in the *Shu-ching*, a Confucianist classic documenting the religious ceremonies of societies that predate the Eastern Chou Era of the eighth to third centuries BCE.

Hsi Wang-mu, the Mother Empress of the West, is also an ancient deity. She is mentioned in the Taoist text *Huai-nan-tzu*, written by a sage of that name in the second century BCE, and in *The Book of Mountains and Rivers (Shang-hai Ching)*, an illustrated collection of mythic geography written before the common era. Other historical records also show that by the third century BCE, the Mother Empress was already a popular deity among the common people. By the time of the Eastern Han period in the first centuries of the common era, she was fully established in the Taoist pantheon.

The Master Who Embraces Simplicity and the even older *Book of the Sage of the Red Pine (Ch'ih-sung Tzu)*, a pre-fourth-century text, both mention the God of the Hearth, or the Kitchen God, who ascends to heaven each month to report on the good and evil deeds of humanity. *The Jade Seal Classic (Yu-ch'ien Ching)*, of the Eastern Han period, specifies the consequences of these reports:

> If you commit a serious misdeed, the Director of Destiny will deduct three hundred years from your life. If you commit a small misdeed, the Director of Destiny will deduct three days from your life.

The Response of the Tao mentions three monsters in our bodies, who also report to the Director of Destiny. Reference to these monsters can be found in *The Master Who Embraces Simplicity*, and the notion that they can block the pathways of energy in the body is elaborated in *Seven Bamboo Strips of the Cloud-Hidden Satchel (Yun-chi Ch'i-ch'ien)*, an encyclopedia of Taoist knowledge compiled in the Northern Sung of the tenth to early twelfth centuries, not long before *The Response of the Tao* itself appeared.

Background of the *Response of the Tao* Stories

The stories of *The Response of the Tao* are not a part of the Taoist canon. They were probably composed by lay teachers of the Action and Karma School to make the teachings of the treatise more accessible to the common person. *The Response of the Tao* itself was written in classical style. The language is terse and the philosophy is expressed in a style of discourse similar to that of the classics. There is no doubt that Li Ying-chang intended to write a philosophical treatise. The stories, however, were written in a more informal style, and were directed towards a more general readership.

The *Response of the Tao* stories can be divided into three categories: those with a strong Taoist influence, those that blend together the beliefs of Buddhism and Taoism, and those that are more Buddhist than Taoist.

The Taoist and Folk Influence

The Taoist stories were probably the earliest of the collection. They were most likely written during the Southern Sung (1127–1279) and the early Ming (1368–1644) periods. Stories that belong to this category are "The Pious Scholar's Fortune", "Charity Rewarded", "The Power of a Good Person's Name", "The North Star Constellation", "Offence Against a Deity", "Ho-kuan and the Ants", and "The Cruel Hunters".

These stories illustrate the basic Taoist belief in reward and retribution presented in *The Response of the Tao* and its predecessor, *The Master Who Embraces Simplicity*. In "Charity Rewarded" and "Ho-kuan and the Ants", those who are kind and compassionate to humans and animals are rewarded. In "The North Star Constellation" and "Offence Against a Deity", those who are disrespectful to the Taoist deities are punished, as are those who kill animals for sport in "The Cruel Hunters".

The deities mentioned in these stories are exclusively Taoist – the Kuan Emperor in "The Scholar's Good Fortune", the Mother Empress of the West (Hsi Wang-mu) in "Charity Rewarded", the Goddess of the Water Realm and Wen-ch'ang Ti-chun in "Offence Against a Deity", the North Star gods and the Thunder God in "The North Star Constellation".

In some of the stories, themes from Taoist folklore form the main story line. "The Power of a Good Person's Name" is probably inspired by the popularity of talismans. Here, the story subtly blends magic and virtue, showing an acceptance of Talismanic Taoism by the Action and Karma School. The story of "The Cruel Hunters" centres around the notion of animal spirits assuming human form, a popular theme in Taoist tales from the T'ang dynasty onwards.

Of these stories, only "The Pious Scholar's Fortune" mentions *The Response of the Tao* explicitly. The rest only allude to the teachings presented in the text. This suggests that by the time the stories were written, *The Response of the Tao* was already a familiar text, and there was no need to mention explicitly the relationship between the text and the stories.

The Taoist and Buddhist Blend

The stories that blend Buddhist and Taoist ideas were probably written during the seventeenth and early eighteenth centuries in the late Ming and early Ch'ing dynasties after the philosophical synthesis of Taoism, Buddhism and Confucianism had become a part of popular thinking. One story, "The God of the Hearth", is set during the reigns of Ming emperors Chia-ching (1522–1566) and Wan-li (1566–1619). Other stories in this group include "The Light of Truth", "A Visit to Hell", "Disrespect for Sacred Texts", and "The Dragon Lord's Wrath". They mark the later phase of development of the Action and Karma School when Buddhism and Taoism were synthesized into a form of popular religion. In these stories, Buddhism and Taoism are integrated with ease. In "The Light of Truth" we are told that *The Response of the Tao* was "inspired by Lao-tzu and compiled by the sages of the Three Religions – Confucianism, Buddhism and Taoism". The Taoist priest who visits the central character of the story blends Taoist and Buddhist ideas naturally when he says, "If the Tao is separated from your heart, your soul will transmigrate through the Six Domains." The Six Domains is a Buddhist term for the hierarchy of existence – ranging from the highest form, the deities, to the lowest form, the demons of Hell. He goes on to say, "If the heart is in union with the Tao, you will be freed from the wheel of samsara and ascend to the realm of immortality." Immortality, a Taoist idea, has been redefined in this story as freedom from reincarnation, showing that by the time this story was written the Buddhist idea of reincarnation was incorporated into Action and Karma Taoism.

In "Disrespect for Sacred Texts", Taoist deities – the Lords of Heaven, Earth and the Water Realm – chastise the students for vandalizing Buddhist texts. They even tell one of them to "give support and protection to the religion of the Buddha" when he becomes a government official. In "A Visit to Hell", a Taoist monk leads the principal character of the story on a tour of Hell. The idea of a tour of Hell is more Buddhist than Taoist; the visit to Hell by a mortal is often used as an eyewitness account, to warn individuals of karmic retribution. In "The God of the Hearth", we are told that after his encounter with the God of the Hearth, Yu-kuang began a new life, adopted the Taoist name Cheng-I Tao-jen, dutifully reported his deeds to this Taoist deity, and invoked the name of the *Bodhisattva* (Buddha-to-be) of Compassion one hundred times every day. Yu – and the author of the story – certainly saw no conflict in paying homage to both Buddhist and Taoist deities.

In "The Dragon Lord's Wrath", Buddhism makes a more subtle appearance; a reference is made to a building project in a Buddhist temple. Why a Buddhist and not a Taoist temple in illustrating the teachings of a Taoist text? A reasonable explanation is that Buddhist temples were more widespread during those times than Taoist temples, and were found even in the smaller towns and villages. The author probably felt that such familiar references would make the story more acceptable. Moreover, this reference suggests that as far as the common people were concerned, there was little difference between a Buddhist and a Taoist shrine.

The Buddhist Influence

In the third group of stories, the influence of Buddhism is stronger than that of Taoism. Stories in this group are "A Bully's Reform", "The Irresponsible Minister" and "Punishment Apportioned to Crime". These stories contain no explicit references to Taoist deities and no mention of Taoism. Rather, the teachings of *The Response of the Tao* are only subtly implied. In "A Bully's Reform", a Buddhist rather than a Taoist story was used to teach the ruffian. In "Punishment Apportioned to Crime", it was not the Taoist deities but Yama, the Buddhist deity of Hell, who punished the wicked man Fan-ch'i. In "The Irresponsible Minister", Wang An-shih mourned his son's death with Buddhist rites and built a Buddhist temple on the site of his son's home.

The Confucian Influence

Although the stories of *Lao-tzu's Treatise on the Response of the Tao* illustrate Taoist and Buddhist teachings, the influence of Confucianism is also strong. In the Southern Sung (twelfth to thirteenth-century) and Ming (fourteenth to mid-seventeenth- century) dynasties, Confucianism experienced a resurgence. There was a renewal of interest in the classics, an almost fanatical reverence for scholarship, and a revival of values such as filial piety, dedication to the state and observance of rules of appropriate social behaviour. In an attempt to stabilize the social structure, the governments of these two dynasties encouraged conservatism and a suspicion of all things foreign. Traditional scholarship was highly valued, and achievement in the civil service was the highest honour a person could attain. These Confucian ideas are woven into many *Response of the Tao* stories. In "The Pious Scholar's Fortune", Shang Shih-yang's reward for his selfless actions is a high literary degree conferred by the emperor. The Kuan Emperor, a Taoist deity, tells Shang to continue to cultivate virtue and to be loyal to his superiors after he has become an official. In "Charity Rewarded", the kind-hearted governor receives a series of promotions. In "A Bully's Reform", the ruffian is rebuked for wasting his talents, being a useless citizen and shaming his parents. In "A Visit to Hell", we are told that scholars whose books have incited people to violence and unethical behaviour are punished severely in Hell. In "Disrespect For Sacred Texts", one student has his punishment lessened because he appeals to a Confucianist value – respect for elders – in defence of his actions. In "Offence Against A Deity", and in "The God of the Hearth", retribution comes in the form of failure in the civil service examinations. On the other hand, reward comes as a government appointment. The Confucianist overtones in the stories allow us to catch a glimpse of the social and intellectual climate of the period and to witness the synthesis of Confucianism, Buddhism and Taoism in popular religion.

Although the *Response of the Tao* stories are not part of the Taoist canon, they are integral to understanding the School of Action and Karma Taoism. Without the stories, the teachings of this School of Taoism probably would not have achieved the popularity they did during the Ming and Ch'ing dynasties. The stories combine philosophy, religion and folk wisdom that appealed to the Chinese populace. Moreover, because the stories of *The Response of the Tao* span more than a hundred years, they provide a valuable insight into the historical development of Action and Karma Taoism.

The Outer Teachings

Lao-tzu's Treatise on the Response of the Tao is regarded as a classic within the Taoist canon. It is not only read by followers of Action and Karma Taoism, but is also highly recommended for study by sects of other schools. Furthermore, *The Response of the Tao* addresses important issues that touch all aspects of our lives. The list of actions described in chapter 6 provides concrete examples of what is considered unethical and harmful to others and ourselves. While some still advocate aggression and competition in the world of business, many are beginning to find that ethics and values have a place in the work and business environment. Honesty and integrity in business practice and respect for employees actually improve performance and productivity. *The Response of the Tao* has much to say about business and work ethics. It advises us not to "say bad things about your co-workers, make your subordinates work so that you can gain favours, criticize others in order to get their position, expose the faults of others to embarrass them, be unkind to subordinates, lie to your supervisors, measure with a false ruler, weigh with a false scale, prosper from unethical dealings".

At a time when crime is one of the most serious problems of society, *The Response of the Tao* teaches that building a crime-free community starts from cultivating the individual. Thus, it teaches us not to "be aggressive and resentful, kill others to get their property and money, use force to get what you want, delight in stealing and grabbing from others, drink and start fights, get involved in gangs and secret societies, steal merchandise, vandalize and set fire to buildings, be violent and injure others".

On the issue of caring for the environment and other sentient life, it tells us not to "shoot animals that fly and run, frighten worms and animals that crawl, fill in burrows and turn over nests, injure young animals and break eggs, bury insects, use poisons to kill trees, waste firewood, hunt in the months of spring, kill turtles and snakes".

Of integrity and honesty in politics, *The Response of the Tao* warns against "taking food meant for refugees, framing the innocent, obstructing civil administration, taking bribes, displaying and using your power unethically, spreading rumours and lies".

Finally, *The Response of the Tao* teaches us to respect others, not to "look down on less fortunate people, ridicule people who are deformed, ridicule those who are retarded" and to be honourable in all actions, not to "take advantage of people who are kind, be dishonest to your relatives, take advantage of widows and orphans, steal skills from others, take property and goods from families who are suffering from misfortune, ruin the livelihood of others, be cruel to people who are kind".

The Inner Teachings

Of all the Taoist scriptures, those of the Action and Karma School are the least esoteric. However, even *Lao-tzu's Treatise on the Response of the Tao* has hidden meanings. These meanings are encoded in Taoist symbolism, and they convey the inner teachings of Action and Karma Taoism. Typically, the inner teachings of a Taoist sect were intended more for the adept follower than the novice. This is because instruction in these teachings requires the practitioner to have understood and incorporated the introductory teachings in his or her everyday life.

The introductory teachings of *The Response of the Tao* can be obtained through a literal reading of the text. It presents a simple and direct relationship between action and consequence. The inner teachings of *The Response of the Tao* present the Action and Karma School's approach to the Taoist idea of cultivating body and mind. The dual cultivation of body and mind is central to Taoist thought. Physical health and spiritual well-being are equally important in Taoist training. Below are three major ideas of the inner teachings of Action and Karma Taoism.

Actions Affect Physical Health and Spiritual Enlightenment

Chapter 2 of *Lao-tzu's Treatise on the Response of the Tao* states that years of life are taken away according to the seriousness of our misdeeds. In the Taoist theory of health and longevity, actions affect states of mind. Self-centred actions such as those prompted by craving and desire create anxiety and tension. Anxiety and tension restrict the flow of blood, cause digestion problems, and prevent the mind from being able to rest peacefully, leading to deterioration of both physical health and mental clarity. Moreover, when the mind is not still, energy cannot gather and circulate. Since Taoism sees the circulation of energy as the prerequisite of good health, actions that disrupt peace of mind will be detrimental to health. In contrast, actions that enhance stillness and clarity of mind will enhance health. When the body is in good health and the mind is empty of desire, enlightenment is attained.

Destructive Actions Hinder the Cultivation of Internal Energy

In chapter 3 it is said that "the Gods of the Three Altars of the North Star watch over us and record our deeds" and "have the power to take away years of our lives according to the seriousness of our misdeeds". It also says that those who "wish to live a long and healthy life should take care and avoid these punishments". The gods of the Three Altar stars are the keepers of the Three Internal Energies in our body: the generative *(ching)*, vital *(ch'i)*, and spirit *(shen)* energy. The three energies are sometimes called the Three Treasures, the Three Herbs, or the Three Flowers. In Taoist symbolism, the Lower Altar Star is the generative energy, the Middle Altar Star the vital energy, and the Upper Altar Star the spirit energy. According to the Taoist theory of health, energy is the basis of health and longevity. Good health is associated with a high level of internal energy and the ease with which the energy can move through the circulatory pathways in the body. Illness is the consequence of the loss of internal energy. Death is the total dissipation of internal energy. Actions in our daily lives affect the level of these energies. Excessive sexual desire drains generative energy. Wild fluctuations of the emotions dissipate vital energy. Planning and scheming for personal gain weaken spirit energy. However, in the same way that egotistic tendencies dissipate energy, selfless action can conserve energy. Consequently, the accumulation of good works can enhance health and longevity.

Negative Attitudes and Emotions Block the Circulation of Energy in the Body

According to *Seven Bamboo Strips of the Cloud-Hidden Satchel*, evil guards or monsters (mentioned in chapter 3 of *The Response of the Tao*) reside in the Three Gates along the *tu* meridian, an energy pathway that runs along the spinal column. The Lower Gate is situated along the spine between the kidneys, the Middle Gate is along the spine between the shoulder blades, the Upper Gate at the point where the spine enters the cranium. The Three Gates are not only associated with the circulation of energy in the tu meridian, but also affect activity in the Three Burning Spaces (the Triple Heater or Three *Tan-t'iens*). The Three Burning Spaces, Upper, Middle and Lower, are involved with the gathering and purification of the spirit, vital and generative energy respectively. The monsters are blockages at the Three Gates. Blockages prevent the circulation of internal energy in the body and hinder the gathering and refining of energy in the Three Burning Spaces. When energy does not circulate smoothly, health will deteriorate.

While negative attitudes and emotions cause blockages in the energy pathways, selfless attitudes and emotions enhance the gathering and circulation of internal energy. Chapter 4 lists the attitudes, emotions and actions that accumulate energy in the body. Chapter 6 lists attitudes, emotions and actions that block and dissipate internal energy. As we spend more time on selfless actions, we have less time for self-centred attitudes, emotions, and behaviour. As a result, the monsters (or blockages) will not develop, energy will circulate, and we will attain a peaceful mind and a healthy body.

Lao-tzu's Treatise on the Response of the Tao offers practical advice on ethical living. Its understanding of the relationship between ethical actions and health and longevity made it one of the most influential Taoist texts ever written. Whether the focus of Taoist training is on internal alchemy, divination, devotion or even magical practices, the foundations of practice are built by developing a disposition toward goodness. Thus, this short treatise contains guidelines for entering the Tao. That is why when asked "What is the entrance into the Tao?" the great Taoist sage and immortal Lü Tung-pin said, "Do good deeds. Be compassionate to all things. Without knowing it, you will have entered the Tao."

Eva Wong

Dates of the Chinese Dynasties

The dynasties waxed and waned in size, sometimes covering different regions, overlapping in time with other dynasties and falling into periods of disarray in which no royal house had control.

HSIA		2205–1765 BCE
SHANG		1766–1121 BCE
CHOU		1122– 225 BCE
Western Chou	1122–770 BCE	
Eastern Chou	770–207 BCE	
Spring and Autumn Period	770–476 BCE	
Warring States Period	475–221 BCE	
CH'IN		221–207 BCE
HAN		206 BCE–219 CE
Western Han	206 BCE–8 CE	
Eastern Han	25–220 CE	
THREE KINGDOMS		220–265 CE
Wei	220–265 CE	
Shu	221–263 CE	
Wu	222–280 CE	
CHIN		265–420 CE
Western Chin	265–316 CE	
Eastern Chin	317–420 CE	
SIX DYNASTIES		420–589 CE
SUI		589–618 CE
T'ANG		618–906 CE
FIVE DYNASTIES AND TEN KINGDOMS		907–960 CE
SUNG		960–1279 CE
Northern Sung	960–1126 CE	
Southern Sung	1127–1279 CE	

CHIN	1115–1234 CE
Y'UAN	1271–1368 CE
MING	1368–1644 CE
CH'ING	1644–1911 CE

BCE: Before Common Era
CE: Common Era

LAO-TZU'S TREATISE ON
THE RESPONSE OF THE TAO

太上曰

CHAPTER ONE

Understanding the Principles

Lao-tzu says:
Fortune and misfortune are the result of our actions.
Reward and retribution follow us like shadows.

刑禍隨

CHAPTER TWO

Words of Warning

There are guardians in Heaven and on Earth
whose job it is to record the misdeeds of each person.
According to the seriousness of these deeds,
years of life are taken away or misfortunes are assigned.
Therefore, those who do evil deeds will meet with retribution.
Prosperity will leave them.
The Baleful Stars will rain disasters on them.
When their years are all taken away from them, they will die.

TRANSLATOR'S NOTE

In Chinese folklore and Taoist belief, there are stars that have a malevolent nature. These Baleful Stars are responsible for natural disasters such as floods, earthquakes, and drought, as well as for personal misfortunes such as death in the family, loss of property, and having unfilial children. The Baleful Stars are countered by the Auspicious Stars which are responsible for good fortune in the family, good harvest, and peaceful times.

錄人罪

CHAPTER THREE

The Guardians

The Gods of the Three Altars of the North Star watch over us
and record our deeds.
They have the power to take away years of our lives
according to the seriousness of our misdeeds.
There are also three [evil] guards residing in our bodies.
During the times of *keng* and *shen*, they ascend to heaven
to report our misdeeds.
At the end of the twelfth lunar month, the God of the Hearth
also reports our actions to the Lords of Heaven.
Those who have committed serious misdeeds
will have their lives taken away.
Those who have committed fewer serious evil deeds
will have years taken away.
Those who wish to live a long and healthy life
should take care to avoid these punishments.

TRANSLATOR'S NOTES

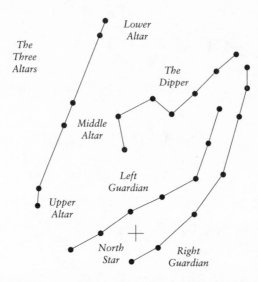

1. According to Chinese astronomy, the North Star Constellation (Dipper) consists of the seven stars of the Dipper, the North Star (ruling star) and two Guardian Star constellations, known as the Left Guardian Formation and the Right Guardian Formation. The principal star in each of the Guardian Formations is known as the Left Guardian and the Right Guardian respectively.

An individual is said to be born under the guardianship of one of the seven stars. His or her health and longevity are linked with the luminosity of his or her birth star in the constellation of the seven stars. Doing evil deeds affects the luminosity of our birth star and thus affects our health and longevity.

The North Star Constellation is also accompanied by three pairs of stars called the Three Altars. The first pair, known as the Lower Altar Stars, are responsible for prosperity. The Middle Altar Stars are responsible for fortune. The Upper Altar Stars are the Guardians of Virtue. It is said that the Three Altar stars are responsible for our birth, growth and protection.

The North Star, the stars of the Dipper, the Guardian Stars and the Altar Stars have power over our lives, granting longevity or taking years from us according to our actions.

2. Keng is one of the ten celestial stems. Shen is one of the twelve terrestrial branches. The celestial stems denote the position of the constellations at the beginning of the new lunar year. The terrestrial branches are commonly used to mark the passage of time divided into fractions of twelve. They mark the

twelve months of the year as well as the twenty-four hours divided into two-hour segments.

The ten celestial stems are *chia, i, ping, ting, wu, chi, keng, hsin, jen, kuei.* The twelve terrestrial branches are *tzu, ch'ou, yin, mao, chen, ssu, wu, wei, shen, yu, hsu, hai.*

The ten celestial stems and twelve terrestrial branches together form the sexagenary (sixty-year) cycle. Each year in this cycle is named after a combination of a celestial stem and a terrestrial branch. For example, the year which starts the sixty-year cycle is called chia tzu, a combination of the first celestial stem, chia, and the first terrestrial branch, tzu. If you line up the ten celestial stems next to the twelve terrestrial branches and keep pairing them until the last stem pairs with the last branch, you will get sixty pairs. The sixty pairs are also used to mark a cycle of sixty days. The days chia tzu and keng shen (the first and fifty-seventh days of each sixty-day cycle) are times in which the (evil) guards report to the Lords of Heaven who evaluate our health and longevity according to the good and bad deeds we have accumulated.

3. The evil guards or monsters in our bodies are also called the Three Worms. They are responsible for illnesses. On the days of chia tzu and keng shen, the doors of heaven are opened and the Jade Emperor asks all spirits, good and evil, to report what they have observed in the human realm during the past sixty-day cycle. The evil guards or worms are delighted to report an individual's evil deeds to the Jade Emperor because as a result of our wrongdoings days of our lives are taken away from us. The sooner the individual dies, the sooner these worms are liberated from the body to become wandering spirits, stealing offerings from temples, graves, and shrines. To eradicate the worms from the body, we must accumulate good deeds. As the internal organs strengthen and internal energy is purified, the worms are destroyed and they can no longer plague the body with illness or create havoc in the spirit world.

4. The God of the Hearth is a subordinate of the Jade Emperor, one of the highest deities in the Taoist pantheon. The God of the Hearth acts as a watch-dog. As a resident in the kitchen and guardian of the stove, he is always around to monitor our activities and report our actions to the Jade Emperor.

11

忠

孝

友

CHAPTER FOUR

Accumulating Good Works

If you are in harmony with the Tao you will advance.
If you are not in harmony with the Tao you will regress.
Do not take the path of evil.
Do not do things in the dark [do not cheat].
Accumulate virtuous deeds and good works.
Be kind and compassionate to all things.
Be dedicated in whatever you do.
Be filial to your parents.
Be harmonious with your siblings and people around you.
Be friendly and helpful to your neighbours.
Use your example of virtuous actions to teach others.
Help orphans and widows.
Respect the old and care for the young.
Do not hurt trees, grass or insects.
Share in the sufferings of others.
Delight in the joys of others.
Help people in desperate need.
Save people from harm.
View the good fortune of others as your good fortune.
View the losses of others as your own loss.
Do not gossip about the faults of others.

Do not boast about your own achievements.
Give much and take little.
Do not complain if you are insulted.
Avoid rewards.
Give and do not expect compensation.
Forget the debts that others owe you.

衆邪遠

CHAPTER FIVE

Reward for Good Deeds

Those who are compassionate are respected by all.
The Way of Heaven will guide and protect them.
Prosperity will follow them.
Evil things will not touch them.
The spirits will guard them.
They will succeed in whatever they do.
They will become immortals.
Those who wish to become immortals in Heaven
should accumulate one thousand three hundred good deeds.
Those who wish to become immortals on earth
should accumulate three hundred good deeds.

侵凌道

CHAPTER SIX

Evil Deeds

These are evil deeds:
Going against the virtue of selflessness.
Being unreasonable.
Using evil intentions to guide your actions.
Being cruel and destructive.
Taking advantage of kind people.
Talking secretly against your parents and elders.
Showing disrespect for your teachers.
Engaging in rebellious actions.
Framing the innocent.
Slandering your co-workers.
Being deceitful.
Lying to your relations.
Being aggressive and resentful.
Taking things for yourself whenever you wish.
Not knowing right from wrong.
Talking behind people's backs.
Making your subordinates work so that you can gain favours.
Being ungrateful for others' help.
Harbouring conflicts and grudges.
Looking down on less fortunate people.

Obstructing civil administration.

Rewarding non-virtuous people.

Punishing people unjustly.

Killing others to acquire their property and money.

Criticizing others in order to acquire their position.

Dismissing good advice.

Taking advantage of orphans and widows.

Taking bribes.

Making what is straight crooked [making what is correct wrong].

Making what is crooked straight [making what is wrong correct].

Making what is light heavy [inflating the seriousness of situations].

Getting angry and killing.

Knowing what is wrong and refusing to correct it.

Knowing what is compassionate and not doing it.

Letting your own wrongdoings mislead others into crime.

Obstructing Taoist teachings.

Insulting the sages and immortals.

Eroding virtuous ways.

Shooting animals that fly and run.

Frightening worms and animals that crawl.

Filling in burrows and turning over nests.

Injuring young animals and breaking eggs.

Wishing that other people would do bad deeds.

Destroying other people's success.

Letting others be exposed to danger so that you can be safe.

Getting rid of others to benefit yourself.

Letting evil replace good.

Letting your private affairs dominate public affairs.

Stealing skills from others.

Ruining the good deeds of others.

Exposing the faults of others to embarrass them.

Stealing others' personal goods.

Stealing merchandise.

Breaking up families.

Taking away someone else's loved ones.

Aiding and abetting crimes.

Displaying and using your power unethically.

Insulting people and being competitive.
Ruining other people's crops and fields.
Breaking up marriages.
Being proud of your riches.
Losing your sense of shame.
Framing other people for crimes.
Buying honour with riches.
Hiding unethical intentions.
Playing down other people's achievements.
Inflating your own small achievements.
Using your power to incriminate others.
Being violent and injuring others.
Cutting corners [short-changing others].
Going against propriety.
Wasting grain.
Annoying good citizens.
Breaking up homes.
Taking property and goods from families suffering from misfortune.
Vandalism and setting fire to buildings.
Obstructing rules and regulations.
Breaking other people's tools and implements so that they cannot use
    them.
Wishing successful people ruin.
Wishing rich people would go bankrupt.
Coveting beautiful and attractive things.
Wishing your creditor would die.
Complaining and fretting if none of the above comes about.
Revealing the faults of others when they are already suffering from
    misfortune.
Ridiculing people who are deformed.
Flattering intelligent people.
Burying insects.
Hating.
Using poison to kill trees.
Making your teachers angry.
Quarrelling with your father and brothers.
Using force to get what you want.

Delighting in stealing and grabbing from others.
Plundering.
Giving rewards and punishments unjustly.
Being boisterous, unruly and without a sense of shame.
Being unkind to subordinates.
Threatening others.
Swearing at Heaven and other people.
Swearing at the wind and rain.
Delighting in arguments and competitions.
Participating in gangs and secret societies.
Listening to the gossip of your spouse and opposing the will of your
    parents.
Forgetting old friends when you have new acquaintances.
Saying one thing and thinking the opposite.
Coveting riches.
Lying to your supervisors.
Spreading rumours and lies.
Framing your subordinates.
Helping guilty parties.
Swearing at the gods.
Going against the harmony and flow of things.
Abandoning your relations.
Saying that the gods are helping you to do unethical deeds.
Not returning what you borrowed.
Asking for much more than is appropriate.
Indulging in excessive sexual desires.
Exhibiting compassion externally and harbouring evil thoughts.
Ruining the livelihood of others.
Leading people astray with false teachings.
Measuring with a false ruler.
Weighing with a false scale.
Mixing the artificial with the real.
Prospering from unethical dealings.
Being cruel to people who are kind.
Ridiculing those who are retarded.
Coveting.
Starting quarrels.

Drinking and starting fights.
Competing with your siblings.
Being an undedicated and dishonest son.
Being an unruly and wild daughter.
Creating conflict in the household.
Not respecting your spouse.
Delighting in boasting.
Being jealous.
Not providing for your spouse and children.
Being rude to your uncles and aunts.
Neglecting your ancestors.
Going against the wishes of your elders.
Committing destructive actions.
Being narrow-minded.
Letting hate and love cloud your judgment.
Swearing at the well and the stove.
Taking food from other people's bowls.
Injuring children and life in the womb.
Engaging in subversive activities.
Carousing on days of chanting.
Being angry on days of the new and full moon.
Facing north when crying and complaining [complaining to the North Star gods].
Crying and mourning at the stove [complaining to the God of the Hearth].
Using fires from the stove to light incense [improper use of fires belonging to the God of the Hearth].
Wasting firewood.
Getting up in the middle of the night naked [see note 1 below].
Slaughtering during harvest festivals.
Cursing at shooting stars.
Pointing at rainbows.
Pointing at the three lights [sun, moon, stars].
Gazing at the sun and moon for long periods.
Hunting during the months of spring.
Facing north while swearing.
Killing turtles and snakes.

TRANSLATOR'S NOTES

1. Taoist sects that advocated the ingestion of substances to attain immortality were very popular during the Eastern Han dynasty (*c*. second century CE). These sects are collectively known as the School of the External Pill, as opposed to the School of the Internal Pill. The School of the Internal Pill (also called the School of Internal Alchemy) believes that the Elixir of Immortality exists within us, and it is through our personal efforts of cultivating the Three Treasures (generative, vital and spiritual energy) that we can attain immortality. The School of the External Pill, on the contrary, believed that immortality could be attained by ingesting minerals, herbs, chemicals and other substances, some of which caused skin rashes. People under the influence of these substances often had to sleep naked so their skin was not irritated by cloth, causing them to scratch the rashes involuntarily during sleep.

2. In traditional China, shooting stars were considered bad omens. If you saw a shooting star, it was said that misfortune would come to you. Cursing at shooting stars amounted to not accepting the misfortune. As suggested in the text, misfortunes are a form of retribution. If we curse retribution, then we are not accepting payment for our misdeeds. As a result we will not sincerely repent of our actions.

3. In general, stars and planets are the residences of deities and should be respected. The North Star is the celestial residence of the Jade Emperor, Guardian of Virtues. To point at the North Star or to expose oneself indecently to the North Star Constellation is to show disrespect for virtues as well as for the guardian star of one's life. (See also note 1, chapter 3.)

水火盗

CHAPTER SEVEN

Retribution for Evil Deeds

If you do these kinds of evil things
then years will be taken from your life,
depending on the seriousness of your evil deeds.
When all the years have been taken from you, you die.
If you have debts, your children and grandchildren
will have to pay them.
If you have taken money and possessions from others,
your spouse and children will suffer the consequences as well;
if your family line is not gradually extinguished,
thieves and robbers will take your possessions;
you will lose them through fire or flood;
you will suffer from illness, in payment for what you have done.
If you kill innocent people,
you will suffer the retribution of violent death.
If you use unethical means to acquire money and possessions,
for example, taking food meant for refugees,
or using liquor to quench your thirst,
not only will you fail to satisfy your hunger,
but you will pay for your actions with death.

起

於

善

CHAPTER EIGHT

Instructions on Important Principles

If the heart is rooted in goodness,
then even before you do a good deed,
the gods of fortune will follow you.
If the heart is rooted in evil,
then even before you do an evil deed,
the gods of misfortune will follow you.

獲吉慶

CHAPTER NINE

Repentance

If you have done evil deeds, repent sincerely.
Do good deeds and refrain from evil deeds in the future.
As time goes on, you will receive due reward.
This is what is meant by turning misfortune into fortune.

故吉人

CHAPTER TEN

Actions

People of good fortune are those who speak what is good,
see what is good
and do what is good.
If you do three good deeds each day,
then, in three years, heaven will shower you with fortune.
Evil people speak what is evil,
see what is evil
and do what is evil.
If you do three evil deeds each day,
then, in three years, heaven will strike you with misfortune.
Pay heed to these teachings and act on them diligently.

THE RESPONSE OF THE TAO
FOLK TALES

Wan Teh-hsu is received by the Lords of Heaven

The Light of Truth

A pious man named Wan Teh-hsu owned a copy of *Lao-tzu's Treatise on the Response of the Tao to Human Actions* and treasured it as a precious heirloom. The book was handed down to him through his grandfather and great-grandfather. Four generations of Wan's family had read the book and practised its teachings diligently. When it came to Wan's generation, he kept the text in a place of honour in the family mansion, and he and his family were especially vigilant in practising the moral principles laid down in the text. Their deeds moved the Lords of Heaven and their actions were recorded in the Book of Life.

One day a Taoist priest visited the home of Wan Teh-hsu. Wan received his guest warmly and presented him with gifts. Being deeply interested in the teachings of the Tao, Wan asked his visitor to enlighten him on subjects such as the Taoist way of living and the methods of health and longevity. The priest began to expound on the nature of the Tao. He said, "The heart is the Tao and the Tao is the heart. If the Tao is separated from the heart, your soul will transmigrate through the Six Domains. You will be trapped in greed, anger and sexual desire. If the heart is in union with the Tao, you will be freed from the wheel of samsara and ascend to the realm of immortality. Unless the Way of Heaven resides in you, no matter how many sacred books you read you will not attain the Tao."

Looking around the room that they were sitting in, the Taoist priest said to his host, "When I first came into your mansion, I noticed a strange glow in your home. You must have a rare treasure in your house. Where do you keep your precious belongings?"

Wan answered, "Taoist master, I am a poor man. There is no treasure of which I can boast."

The priest led Wan Teh-hsu to the very place where the *The Response of the Tao to Human Actions* was kept. Pointing to the book, he said, "This book is the treasure. It was inspired by Lao-tzu himself and compiled by the sages of the Three Religions – Confucianism, Buddhism, and Taoism. This book describes the path of virtue that each individual should follow in his or her lifetime. If a person follows the teachings of the book without seeking personal gain, every word will radiate brightness. If a person practises the teachings with a secret desire for reward, no trace of light will be visible, for the darkness of greed will have covered its native glow.

"Your good deeds have illuminated the book and its brightness has reached the realm of heaven. Your heart and your actions are harmonious with the will of the Lord of Heaven. I can assure you that you will attain immortality. However, you must not let this lower your vigilance. Keep in sight the heavenly reward that awaits you. Continue to exercise discipline in your interactions with your fellow human beings and do not fail to complete the work that you have begun."

Wan Teh-hsu took the words of the Taoist priest to his heart and practised the teachings of *The Response of the Tao* with even greater zeal. For thirty more years he did everything he could to benefit others and to promote the welfare of his community. One day Wan's neighbours heard music from the skies and saw a host of celestial beings. They looked again and saw Wan and his family, along with the immortals, being carried up to Heaven on a cloud in broad daylight. Later, the villagers built a shrine on Wan's land to remember him. It was said that those who petitioned the immortal Wan Teh-hsu with a sincere heart did not fail to have their wishes granted.

TRANSLATOR'S NOTES

1. The Book of Life is a roster of names kept in the court of the Jade Emperor, Guardian of Virtues and one of the highest deities in the Taoist pantheon. It is said that subordinates of the Jade Emperor, such as the God of the Hearth, report individuals' good and evil deeds to the Jade Emperor. The Jade Emperor examines the records and adds years to, or strikes years from, the lives of individuals according to the balance of their good and evil deeds. Those who are awarded longevity are said to have their names listed in the Book of Life. Those who are punished are said to have their names listed in the Book of Death. The judgment is then carried out by Wen-ch'ang Ti-chun (Patron of the Arts and Literature), the immediate subordinate of the Jade Emperor.

2. In Chinese Mahayana Buddhism, there is a hierarchy of existence called the Six Domains. The domains are, from highest to lowest: deities, humans, animals, *ausuras* (warlike demons), hungry ghosts, and Hell denizens. Reincarnation into any one of these existences will depend on the number of good deeds one has accumulated in the preceding life.

The pious scholar Shang Shih-ying is introduced to the Emperor

The Pious Scholar's Fortune

In the Ming dynasty (1368–1644) there lived a talented calligrapher by the name of Shang Shih-ying. Though poor, Shang was very virtuous. When he saw a man asking for help to print and distribute *Lao-tzu's Treatise on the Response of the Tao to Human Actions* he wanted to support the man's endeavour. However, he had no money so he decided to pawn his clothes. This left Shang with no warm clothing in the winter. But his personal sacrifice made the publication of the text possible.

Fortune did not come to Shang even when he was thirty years old. He went to the capital, hoping that his luck would turn, but no one recognized his abilities. To earn a living, he took a job at a small shrine as copier and writer of poems dedicated to the Kuan Emperor, a Taoist deity.

When New Year's Eve was approaching, the chief magistrate of the district had some official business at the shrine of the Kuan Emperor. He sent one of his clerks, a cultured man who appreciated good art, to take care of the business. When the clerk saw Shang's calligraphy on the inscriptions in the hall, he was greatly impressed and invited the poor scholar to his home as a guest.

Later that month at the Festival of Lanterns, the chief magistrate was having his garden decorated with lanterns, in the spirit of the event. It was also customary to have poems written spontaneously and inscribed on the lanterns. Many poets and calligraphers were there, testing their skills and competing with each other. However, none of the scholars present could produce anything that satisfied the magistrate. The clerk remembered his calligrapher friend and recommended Shang to his superior.

Shang was summoned to the magistrate's residence and his talents impressed all who were there. That evening, the Emperor paid his minister a visit and was greatly taken by Shang's calligraphy. He had Shang presented to him and conferred on him a high literary degree. From then on, fortune smiled on Shang. The Emperor promoted him and, before long, Shang received the highest literary honour – he was made the Emperor's personal secretary.

One day, after his work at the court was finished, Shang went to the shrine of the Emperor Kuan to give thanks for his fortune and prosperity. The priest received him as a guest of honour and invited him to spend an evening there. That night, the Emperor Kuan himself appeared before Shang and said, "The fortune that you are enjoying today is the consequence of your efforts in helping others print and distribute *Lao-tzu's Treatise on the Response of the Tao to Human Actions*. Continue to cultivate virtue. Be loyal to your superiors. Be dedicated in your service to the country. Do not abuse your power and continue to do good work."

It was said that Shang continued to live a virtuous life and advised others to do the same. In this way, he led many people to the path of virtue.

TRANSLATOR'S NOTES

1. The Kuan Emperor was Kuan Yu, an historical figure who lived during the Period of the Three Kingdoms in the Kingdom of Shu. Kuan Yu helped Lui Pei in his battle against T'sao T'sao, a minister of the late Eastern Han dynasty with imperial ambitions. Known for his integrity and strength of character, Kuan Yu soon became the popular symbol of the virtues of uprightness and personal sacrifice, and was elevated to the status of a folk hero. Later it was said that Kuan's actions so impressed the Lords of Heaven that he was deified after his death and given the title "Kuan-ti", the Emperor Kuan. He became the patron of the martial arts and guardian of the virtues of justice,

dedication, uprightness, and personal sacrifice. As a deity he continued to do great deeds in the service of the Lords of Heaven, battling against evil spirits and gods fallen under evil influence. Because of his accomplishments in the immortal realm, he was elevated to a high rank within the pantheon, eventually becoming the Jade Emperor.

2. In Chinese tradition, the lunar new year is a time of festivities and celebration. On New Year's Eve, it is customary for the family to visit the local flower festival and buy seasonal flowers to welcome the new year.

The lunar new year Festival of Lanterns falls on the fifteenth day (full moon) of the first month and marks the start of the first of the three Taoist seasons. The second season begins on the fifteenth day of the seventh month. The third season begins on the fifteenth day of the tenth month. The first season is ruled by the Lord of Heaven and his birthday falls on the Festival of Lanterns. The second season is ruled by the Lord of Earth and the third season is ruled by the Lord of the Waters. It is said that the Lord of Heaven grants prosperity, the Lord of Earth forgives wrong-doing, and the Lord of the Waters protects us from suffering and disaster. Therefore, in conjunction with the celebration of the new year, people also celebrate the birthday of the Lord of Heaven and ask him to grant fortune and prosperity to their family for the new year. In addition to hanging lanterns, special ceremonies for the Lords of the Three Seasons are performed.

The origin of the Lanterns Festival can be dated to the Han dynasty in the first century. It is believed that the festival evolved from a ceremony in which the Han emperors sacrificed to a god called the Ancient One. In the Historical Records, Ssu-ma Ch'ien describes a ceremony in which the Han emperor gazed at the sky from sunset to sunrise. Since the ceremony took place throughout the night, many lanterns were lit to illuminate the sacrificial area. People began to gather to see the splendour of the spectacle and gradually the ceremonies became an event for the populace as well as the nobility.

The benevolent governor is attended by immortals

Charity Rewarded

For some reason, the people of Chang-hsi province did not want to raise daughters. As a result, women were rare and there was an unusual number of bachelors in that district. When the governor investigated the matter, he found that many female infants were drowned at birth. Being a kind-hearted man, he wanted to put an end to this inhumane practice. He summoned his councillors to consider what measures could be taken to discourage this activity. Old state records were examined and it appeared that attempts had been made by previous governors to halt the practice, but none succeeded.

After meeting with the councillors, the governor retired to his study, still thinking that there must be a way to end such cruelty. All day thoughts ran through his mind. "What is it that makes people suppress parental love? It must be that they cannot afford the dowry and marriage expenses. If we build a public nursery so that the female children can be provided for by the state, then the drowning may stop."

That night the governor looked through the treasury records and found that there were deserted temples and shrines at which an annual tax was still being collected. It occurred to him that such revenue could be used to fund and maintain nurseries. He resolved to go to the temple of Hsi Wang-mu [the Mother Empress of the West] in the morning and ask for advice and assistance in this project.

That same night the priest of the temple had a dream in which the Mother Empress appeared, informing him of the charitable intentions of the governor and his impending visit. She also told him that, although the project was still in the planning stages, the compassion which inspired it had moved the Lords of Heaven. Already a host of immortals had been sent to attend to the governor's needs.

As commanded by the Mother Empress, the priest made all the necessary preparations to receive the governor. In the morning, the governor arrived at the temple. After the reception ceremony, the priest asked the governor if he was planning to build a nursery for female children. The governor was surprised and asked the priest how he had learned of his idea. He had only devised the plan the night before and had not discussed it with anyone. The priest then told the governor of his dream and his meeting with the Mother Empress of the West.

With the help of the temple administration and intervention from the deities, the governor's benevolent plan was carried out successfully. Not only were the people happy with the outcome of the events, but the district enjoyed a prosperity never seen before. The governor himself received a series of promotions from the emperor and lived to an advanced age, surrounded by several generations of descendants who were all prosperous and respected.

TRANSLATOR'S NOTES

1. In Chinese tradition, marriage expenses were almost entirely covered by the bride's family. These include the house, the furniture (except the bed, which was provided by the groom's family), jewellery, clothing for the bride, and the cost of the wedding banquet.

2. Hsi Wang-mu, or the Mother Empress of the West, is both a folklore figure and a Taoist deity. First mentioned by Lieh-tzu, a Taoist writer of the fourth and fifth century BCE, Hsi Wang-mu was said to be formed of the Primordial Vapour of the West. She embodies the yin principle (the west being associated with yin and the east with yang) and is the ruler of the Western Heavenly Realm.

With the introduction of Buddhism to China and later developments of Taoist thought, the Mother Empress of the West became the Guardian of the

Western Realm of Heaven, the Lands of Immortality. To those who accumulated good deeds in their lifetime, she opened the gate of the Western Lands of Immortality. As the folklore of Buddhism and Taoism became more intertwined, she became synonymous with Kuan-yin, the Bodhisattva (Buddha-to-be) of compassion. Both figures are said to dwell in the Immortal Realm of the West. Both are patrons of compassion, and both intercede for mortals to deliver them from suffering.

The Power of a Good Person's Name

King-shing was a virtuous man. While journeying through a district called Chun-h'ua, he stayed with a family whose young daughter was possessed by evil spirits. The spirits tormented the girl daily but, when King-shing was in the house, the demons were afraid to enter.

The next day, when King-shing left, the evil spirits returned. The young girl asked them why they did not come the day before. The demons answered, "We are afraid of the man called King-shing." The girl quickly told her father about this and the father immediately ran after King-shing to call him back.

When King-shing heard the father's plea, he said, "I do not need to be there physically to ward off the demons." He took a slip of paper and wrote the following words on it: "King-shing is here." Then he told the father, "Paste this slip of paper on your door and the spirits will not bother you again."

The father did what he was told and from that day onward the girl was free from the influence of the demons. This story shows that the very name of a virtuous person can chase away evil spirits.

TRANSLATOR'S NOTE

The power of names is associated with the magical power of talismans. The name is written in a special script that invokes power. Talismans can draw power from names of deities and from very virtuous people. The popularity of talismans dates back to the rise of a popular sect of Taoism known as the Dragon-Tiger sect in the Eastern Han dynasty during the second century. Its founder, Chang Tao-liang, was said to have cured sickness and warded off disasters with talismans that invoked the names of the deities.

The bully is reprimanded by the old gentleman

A Bully's Reform

Wu Ch'ien-ch'iu of Shan-yu was extraordinarily strong. No one in his town could best him in boxing or sword-play. He was overbearing in his behaviour and used his strength to intimidate others. He made sure that anyone who opposed him paid for it. He borrowed property and never returned it. He forced people to do things for him under threat of severe punishment.

One summer evening, he went to the tower above the city gate to enjoy the cool breeze. When he arrived, everyone fled except one old gentleman. The old man remained there, oblivious to Wu's presence.

Wu was annoyed. He was not accustomed to people who dared to defy him. Intending to intimidate the old man, Wu said gruffly, "Why do you dare ignore me? Are you trying to defy my power?"

The old gentleman replied sternly, "How ignorant you are! Your mother carried you in her womb for ten months. She fed you and cared for you for three years. Your parents hoped that you would become a prominent citizen and bring respect to the family. But now look at you! You have wasted your talents and degraded yourself by turning into a bully. The country loses in you a useful citizen. Your parents are put to shame by your behaviour. You should pity yourself!"

Hearing the old man's words, Wu was drenched in a cold sweat. He declared, "Everyone saw me as an undesirable character, so I became

53

one. Your words have woken me up. Please tell me what I should do to repair the damage that has been done to my family's name."

The gentleman replied, "You must have heard the story of the butcher who threw away his knife and became a Buddhist. Follow his example. Start a new life and set your old ways behind you. From now on become a virtuous man and you will command the respect of others."

Wu took the old man's advice at once. He joined the army and used his strength to help instead of harm. Eventually he was promoted to the rank of general and won wide respect.

TRANSLATOR'S NOTE

The Buddhist tale referred to by the old gentleman is about a butcher who had a shop in the market place across the street from a Buddhist temple. Daily the butcher slaughtered animals and sold the meat, while the scriptural chanting for compassion toward all living things drifted across the street each morning and evening. Years went by, and the butcher seemed untouched by the message. However, one day he received a pregnant sow in a delivery. As he was about to slaughter the pig, the Buddhist chants came to his mind. He dropped the knife in horror and said to himself, "If I kill the sow, I will have taken not one life but many. All my life I have killed and not valued the lives of sentient beings. Now, I shall give up my trade, stop the killing, and become a follower of the Buddha." The butcher closed his shop, set his animals free and went into the Buddhist temple to become a monk. It was said that the Buddha, who saw this happen, told his attendants, "No matter how many crimes a person has committed, if he sincerely repents and abandons the wrong ways, he can attain enlightenment."

Minister Wang An-shih is tortured in Hell

The Irresponsible Minister

Minister Wang An-shih was a learned scholar but he was also reckless and irresponsible. Without proper consideration of the consequences, he introduced radical reforms in the administration of the Northern Sung dynasty that upset the welfare of the people. The citizens complained and the officials objected. Even the emperor was surprised and annoyed by his minister's outrageous policies. But, against all advice, Wang defended his actions and declared, "Heavenly omens have no meaning and popular discontent should be ignored. There is no sense in following outdated rules."

With the assistance of his son, a magistrate, Wang attempted to reintroduce bodily mutilation and castration as a punishment. However, before the law was passed, his son died and Wang An-shih built a Buddhist temple where his son had lived. While performing the Buddhist rites for the dead, Wang thought he saw an image of his son in the candle flame. Bound in fetters, the son cried to him, "Our attempt to revive the punishment of bodily mutilation angered the Lords of Heaven. I am doomed to suffer infernal torment forever."

Later Wang An-shih fell from grace in the imperial court. He lost his ministerial post and died miserably in exile. Not long after his death, one of his relations fell seriously ill and became unconscious for a short time. When the man recovered, he said that he had been taken into a region of Hell. The entrance was marked by a sign that read "Wickedness and Crime Eternally Prohibited Here". There he saw a noble-looking man with grey hair and large eyes in a wooden body restraint. Though he did not mention the name of this unfortunate individual, everyone knew that it was Wang An-shih. When Wang's daughter asked what could be done to alleviate her father's suffering, the sick man simply said, "Do charitable works and accumulate merit. That is all."

TRANSLATOR'S NOTE

Wang An-shih was a minister of the Northern Sung Period (960–1127). According to historical records, he was not the villain portrayed in this story. Before becoming adviser to the emperor, Wang An-shih was respected by both the scholarly community and the common people. It was his reputation as a just and dedicated official that made him a minister and adviser to the emperor. While in office, Wang was a conscientious minister and introduced reforms intended to strengthen the borders of the Sung Empire, promote literacy, increase revenue for the central government, public works and the defence budgets, and combat crime through increased emphasis on law and order. However, many of Wang's plans were impractical intellectual ideals. Moreover, corruption in the government prevented their effective implementation. As a result, the people's lives became more difficult than they were before the reforms were instituted. In the five years during which the reforms were carried out, the popularity of Wang An-shih fell and he came to be seen as the epitome of evil. The story probably comes from a time when the memories of Wang An-shih's disastrous reforms were still very much alive and the resentment against him was still strong.

Ch'uan Ju-yu visits Hell

A Visit to Hell

Ch'uan Ju-yu of Pu-hai was a poor man but, instead of striving to become rich, he spent his time helping others. Despite the bad health that dogged him, he worked long and hard copying religious books to distribute to his neighbours. When asked why he stretched himself to the limit, Ch'uan replied that he was not seeking any reward; he was simply trying to keep his mind from being idle.

One day when Ch'uan was at sea, a great storm shipwrecked him on a lonely but beautiful island. Ch'uan was immersed in the splendour of his surroundings when a Taoist sage appeared and said to him, "The mortal world delights in hypocrisy and the sensational. But the Lords of Heaven praise those who are sincere. You have done good by copying and distributing books that teach virtue. Moreover, you did this not to gain reward or praise but purely out of goodwill. Many scholars are learned but they abuse their talents. They write books that incite people to violence and non-virtuous acts. They are now suffering in the inferno of Hell as a consequence of their deeds. I shall take you there so that you can see how different your own fate is."

The Taoist took Ch'uan to a strange land and thoroughly explained what Ch'uan witnessed there. Ch'uan saw the various tortures suffered by writers who led people into violence and were responsible for the downfall of otherwise good people. The sage also pointed out a stately gentleman who had been an upright and just magistrate during his earthly life. He was now in charge of justice in the underworld, ensuring that those who erred in their life on earth would be punished in Hell.

When the visit was over, the Taoist returned Ch'uan to the desert island where he eventually managed to build a boat and return home to his village. Deeply affected by his visit to Hell, Ch'uan went around telling everyone of the terrible scenes he had witnessed. He advised them to lead a virtuous life so that they would not face such punishments after their death.

TRANSLATOR'S NOTE

In Chinese folklore, Hell was originally seen as a kind of underworld where demons and the dead dwell. The idea of punishment in Hell as retribution for evil deeds is Buddhist in origin and the eye-witness account of a tour of Hell is a common theme in many Buddhist moral tales used to warn individuals of karmic retribution.

Disrespect for Sacred Texts

In the district of Wu K'ung-hien there was a temple with a library which was open to students from the local schools. One winter day, four of the students used some of the sacred books for heating fuel and another one burned a book to warm the toilet. Another member of the group, K'ang Tui-shan, disapproved of their conduct, but was afraid to say anything.

The next night K'ang Tui-shan dreamt that he and his fellow students were hauled before the Lords of Heaven, Earth and the Water Realm. One of the deities said to them, "Buddha is a great being. Why have you dared to burn his books to warm yourselves?"

The four students who used the books for heating fuel at once prostrated themselves. They begged for pardon but the lords condemned them to death. The one who burned a book to warm the toilet was told he would never receive any advancement in his life. Finally, the lords asked K'ang Tui-shan why he had not voiced his disapproval of his friends' actions. K'ang replied, "I knew what they did was wrong, but they are my elders. I was afraid my reproaches would be disrespectful."

"In that case," said the deity, "you are pardoned. But, when you have advanced to a prominent position in the government, remember to support and protect the religion of the Buddha."

When K'ang awoke the next morning he recorded his dream. Everything came to pass as he had dreamed. Years later, he obtained the degree of first rank in the civil service examination and received a prestigious appointment. The other four students failed and were not given an opportunity to re-sit, for, six months later, they and their families all perished in a plague. The student who burned a book to heat the toilet was a poor schoolmaster to the end of his days. Eventually, he died of starvation in the seventh year of the reign of Shih-sung of the Ming dynasty [c.1529].

TRANSLATOR'S NOTE

In the Taoist pantheon, the Lords of Heaven, Earth, and the Water Realm are the immediate subordinates of Wen-ch'ang Ti-chun, the first officer of the Jade Emperor. When the Jade Emperor decrees reward or punishment, the judgment is generally proclaimed by Wen-ch'ang Ti-chun and carried out by the Lords of Heaven, Earth, and the Water Realm. These deities are sometimes portrayed as police captains and are given power to carry out punishment or give reward on the spot.

The Lord of Heaven is also known as the Bringer of Prosperity, the Lord of the Earth as the Forgiver of Wrongs and the Lord of the Water Realm as the Deliverer from Suffering. They have the power to award prosperity, forgive wrongs in the light of repentance, and cause or prevent natural disasters. (See also note on p.39.)

Punishment Apportioned to Crime

Fan-ch'i led a life of crime in the city of Hsi Shui-suan. He instigated violence, stirred up quarrels, seized the property of others by force, and seduced other men's wives and daughters. When he could not get what he wanted, Fan devised the most dishonourable schemes to obtain it.

One day he died suddenly. Twenty-four hours later he was back and instructing his wife to gather his relations and neighbours at his mansion. When they arrived, he announced that he had seen the Lord of the Underworld who said to him, "In my realm the dead receive punishment according to their crimes. Those in the realm of the living do not know what is in store for them. When they die they will be thrown into flames whose heat is in proportion to the harm they have done to their fellow human beings."

The crowd looked at Fan-ch'i as if he was babbling nonsense. But Fan-ch'i had more than filled his measure of crime, and the Lord of the Underworld had decided to use him as an example to deter the people from evil deeds. At his command, Fan-ch'i took a knife and began mutilating himself. With each slash, he recited a crime that he had committed against his family and neighbours.

The rumour of Fan-ch'i's actions spread and many people came to see the mangled body of the tormented man. In grief and shame, his wife and children tried to close the door to keep out the curious crowd. However, the power of the Lord of the Underworld was still in Fan-ch'i. He struggled to speak to his family saying, "I am carrying out the orders of the Lord of the Underworld who wants my punishment to serve as a warning to others. You have no right to prevent them from seeing my ordeal."

Fan-ch'i lived in agony for six more days before he finally died.

TRANSLATOR'S NOTE

The Lord of the Underworld is also called Yen-huang, after Yama, a Buddhist deity of Hell. Just as the Lords of Heaven oversee the condition of humanity, the Lords of Hell govern the world of the dead. Yama, Lord of the Underworld, has supreme power over the souls of the dead. Far from being a malevolent deity, Yama is considered a just ruler, meting out punishments to fit the crimes committed during one's lifetime.

P'ang Heng-hsiu prostrates himself before the deities of the North Star Constellation

The North Star Constellation

P'ang Heng-hsiu and his friends organized a group dedicated to worshipping the deities of the North Star Constellation. He observed all the rites and chanted the scriptures with devotion.

But one day P'ang drank too much and became intoxicated. That night, he stripped naked and fell asleep facing north, thereby showing disrespect for the deities of the North Star Constellation. In the middle of the night, he woke and urinated facing north. A loud crack of thunder brought him to his senses and, shocked at his nakedness, he hastily put on his clothes. As he hurriedly prostrated himself to pay homage to the deities, he saw a god with a dark face and dragon-like whiskers standing over him. The deity carried a golden rod and spoke sternly to P'ang: "You are the leader of a religious group and you are well aware of the rules and regulations. You should receive double punishment for your disrespect toward the North Star deities."

P'ang begged for mercy, saying that he was temporarily under the influence of alcohol and not his usual self. The god said, "Good people never relax their vigilance. Do you remember the story of Ch'u Pai-yu? When he passed the royal palace at night he dismounted from his carriage to pay his respects to the emperor even when no one was there. People are still praising his sincerity and propriety. Therefore, in the dark night you should not yield to shameful behaviour. We will let you go now, but you must suffer the consequences later in the form of a court punishment."

After that, P'ang was afraid to leave his house lest he encounter misfortune. But how could a mortal escape punishment decreed by the will of heaven? One day, P'ang received an invitation to visit a relation who had recently been promoted to a prominent position in the imperial court. He accepted the invitation gladly and set off for the capital. On his arrival, he spent time recklessly enjoying the city. He passed by an imperial shrine and, not knowing its significance, did not stop to pay his respects. He was immediately arrested by the guards of the shrine for the offence and hauled before the magistrate's office. His punishment was one hundred lashes. It was then that P'ang realized that the prophecy of his punishment was fulfilled.

TRANSLATOR'S NOTES

1. The North Star Constellation (the Dipper) is said to be the celestial residence of the stars of longevity with the North Star itself as the home of the Jade Emperor (see note 1, chapter 3, p.8).

In Devotional Taoism, the North Star deities are worshipped by chanting the Liturgy of the North Star on the first and fifteenth days of the lunar month, on one's birthday, and from the first to the ninth day of the ninth lunar month. On this last occasion, the deities of the North Star descend to earth to observe humanity and send their reports back to the Jade Emperor. The chanting of the North Star Liturgy is also quite popular among lay believers. Regular chanting, observance of the North Star festival, and respect for the North Star deities are said to bring prosperity and longevity. Disrespect, however, will bring retribution.

The North Star Constellation also symbolizes the nature of the Tao. The North Star itself does not change its position and so is like the unchanging and permanent aspect of the Tao that is the underlying reality of all existence. The other stars in the constellation revolve around the North Star symbolizing the dynamic, changing aspect of the Tao. They are the adaptability of the Tao to circumstances.

The symbolism of the North Star and the stars in the Constellation can also be said to embody the Taoist concepts of health, longevity, and virtue. Many liturgies and treatises on the arts of longevity have been based on the North Star Constellation. Reverence for the North Star Constellation, whether as deity or symbol, is shared by all major Taoist sects.

2. The story contains a literal interpretation of the reference in chapter 6 of *The Response of the Tao* to "getting up in the middle of the night naked". An alternative interpretation to this, relating it to the practices of the School of the External Pill, is offered in the notes for chapter 6 (p.20). The more literal interpretation in the story suggests that the tales date from a time when the practices of the External Pill were not part of Taoist training.

The Goddess of the Water Realm punishes the student

Offence Against a Deity

The village of Ch'ing Ch'i had a shrine dedicated to the Goddess of the Water Realm in which the statue of the goddess was so beautiful that everyone agreed she looked as if she were alive. The villagers made her the guardian of their district and paid her homage and respect.

In the second month of the year, when the pear blossoms were in bloom, a group of young students passed the shrine on their way to view the flowers. They entered the shrine and one of them lifted the curtain hanging over the altar of the goddess. "How beautiful she is," he exclaimed. "If she was alive I'd surely make her my mistress." His friends were shocked at his outrageous remark but he laughed at them and said, "Gods and spirits are not real. People who believe in them are superstitious." He then scribbled a libellous poem on the wall. Knowing that he would never listen to them, his friends refrained from giving further advice.

Later that year, the students went to the capital to take the civil examinations. While staying in a dormitory named after the Lord Wen-ch'ang, Patron of the Arts and Literature, they all had the same dream. In the dream, Lord Wen-ch'ang appeared to them and they were awed by his majesty. The deity took a scroll, rolled it out on the table and declared, "As you all know, any student who is guilty of being disrespectful to women will be excluded from the list of honour. Even an ordinary woman should be respected, not to mention a goddess. It has come to my attention that one of you has insulted the Goddess of the Water Realm in a shrine in the village of Ch'ing Ch'i." As he named the offender, he struck his name from the list of honour, emphasizing that this was done because the student was disrespectful to a woman.

When the students awoke the next morning and discovered they had all had the same dream, the offender scoffed at the warning, asking, "Why would the Lord of the Arts and Literature get involved with this matter? What harm can a clay image do?"

He strode into the examination room and wrote his essays with his usual brilliance, confident of his success. But, that evening, the Goddess of the Water Realm appeared with her attendants. She rebuked him for his offence and his impertinence and ordered her maids to strike him with their sticks. The student lost his mind and destroyed all his writings. The next morning the scholar was found lying unconscious on the floor. He was carried out of the room and died soon afterwards.

TRANSLATOR'S NOTES

1. T'ien K'ou, the Goddess of the Water Realm, is one of the incarnations of Hsi Wang-mu, Mother Empress of the West. Hsi Wang-mu is also known as the Golden Mother of the Tortoise. The Tortoise is the god Y'uan-wu, Lord of the Northern Quadrant. The element water is associated with the direction North and the Tortoise is said to emerge from the depths of the ocean to bring the divinational arts to humanity. As the myths evolved, the Mother Empress of the West became the female counterpart of Y'uan-wu and both deities were adopted by sea-going people as the patrons of seafarers and protectors of fishermen and sailors.

2. Wen-ch'ang Ti-chun (Lord Wen-ch'ang) is the immediate subordinate of the Jade Emperor. His function is to pronounce reward or punishment as decreed by the Jade Emperor. As the Patron of the Arts and Literature, he has the domain of scholastic achievement as his special concern. Therefore, he is often portrayed as the ruler of the destiny of scholars.

The God of the Hearth

During the Ming dynasty in the reign of the emperor Chia-ching, an unusually gifted man named Yu-kuang lived in the province of Kiang-shih. Yu acquired an education that showed both depth and variety of learning. At the age of sixteen he received the primary degree required for entry into the civil service. He excelled in his studies and passed all the examinations with distinction. But when he reached the age of thirty he found that he was beset with one misfortune after another and had to make his livelihood by tutoring.

At about this time, Yu joined several other scholars in offering homage to Wen-ch'ang Ti-chun, Patron of the Arts and Literature. He carried out charitable works dutifully. He guarded against the misuse of book paper, freed captive animals and refrained from slanderous speech. To all appearances he was a virtuous man. But there was no sign of reward. In fact, he failed the examination for the secondary degree seven times.

Yu married and had five sons. However, four of the sons fell seriously ill and died very young. The last son, a boy of rare intelligence and charm, had two black spots on the sole of his left foot. This child was the favourite of his parents, but one day, when he was eight years old, he lost his way while playing in the street. He disappeared and was never seen again. Yu had four daughters but three died in their

81

teens. His wife lost her sight weeping for her children. The family's misery increased as the years went by. Yu began to wonder if his behaviour had in some way angered the Lords of Heaven. He examined his actions carefully but could find nothing that he thought could have offended the deities. Despondent, he resigned himself to fate, but not without murmuring against the injustice that was forced on him.

When he reached forty, Yu began to write a petition to the God of the Hearth at the end of each year, asking the deity to carry his messages to the Lords of Heaven. For several years Yu dutifully wrote his petition on a yellow slip of paper and burned it on the last day of the twelfth month. Several years passed, and no response came.

When he was forty-seven years old, he spent New Year's Eve with his blind wife and their only surviving daughter. Sitting together in a room with few belongings, the three tried to console each other in the face of their misfortune. Suddenly, there was a knock at the door. Yu took the lamp, opened the door, and saw an old man with silvery hair and a long white beard. The strange man wore a black robe and a square black hat. He entered, bowed slightly to Yu, and said, "My name is Ch'ang. I have travelled a long way to your home because I have heard your petitions. I hope to offer you some comfort in your distress."

Yu was astonished and respectfully returned the bow. He said, "Sir, all my life I have tried to be virtuous, but to this day I have not received advancement. Most of my children have died. My wife has become blind and we barely earn enough to stay alive. For the past seven years I have made offerings and petitions to the God of the Hearth without fail. I don't know what I have done to cause this misfortune."

Ch'ang replied, "For many years I have watched your actions. You have entertained many evil thoughts. You were empty in your so-called virtuous actions. Your offerings to the Lords of Heaven were insincere. In your heart you murmur and accuse the lords for their unfair treatment of you. For this you face further retribution."

Yu was both frightened and surprised at the old man's words. He protested, "Sir, I have heard that in the realm of Heaven, each person's deeds are recorded in meticulous detail, and reward and retribution are given accordingly. All my life I have tried to do good works. I have tried to follow the rules and regulations of good behaviour laid down by the sages. How can it be said that I did my good deeds simply for display?"

Ch'ang said, "My friend, among the precepts there is one concerning respect for the written words of the sages. You claim to guard the written word, but you let your fellow students and pupils misuse the leaves of the ancient books. They made envelopes and wiped their desks with them. They then made excuses, saying it did not matter that the paper was soiled since it would be burned immediately. This happened regularly before your eyes and yet you said nothing. How can you say that you have followed the regulations properly when you did not correct the wrongs of others?"

The old man continued, "It is true that every month you set free captive animals, but you merely followed what others did. When no one was there to set an example, you faltered in your decision. Compassion has not spontaneously arisen in your heart. You cut the throats of lambs and boil lobsters alive for your dinner without considering that they too are endowed with the breath of life.

"As for slanderous speech, you have committed more acts of libel than could be enumerated. You took pride in your reason and force of argument. You never failed to silence those who were slower in their thinking. You disputed with everyone around you, hurting their feelings and losing their friendship. You took advantage of your forcefulness and taunted others so that no one felt comfortable in your presence. For this, you have angered the deities. Your offences were recorded in Heaven and, although you regarded yourself as virtuous, your thoughts and actions did not deceive me or my superiors in Heaven.

"It is true that you have not actively committed crimes but, when you saw someone's property and wanted it, you committed the crime of stealing. When you saw another man's wife and desired her, you committed the crime of rape. Think over your thoughts. Do you have the discipline of the sage Lu Nan-tzu? One night the sage was obliged to find shelter in the house of a widow. He lit the lamp in his room and read the classics aloud all night to avoid arousing her suspicion and causing her discomfort. You think that you have been blameless and that you can present yourself without fear before the Lords of Heaven and the Guardians of Hell. All this time you have deceived yourself.

"I have presented your petitions to the Lords of Heaven. However, in all the years that I have been charged to watch your thoughts and actions, I could not find a virtue worth recording. You have nothing in your heart but thoughts of vice, envy, selfishness, pride, scorn, ambition, hate, anger, ingratitude, and cruelty. These thoughts have accumulated daily so that even I could not keep track of them all. The Lords of Heaven have recorded many of your evil deeds. You will receive further punishment in due course. Misfortune will follow you all your life."

The old man finished speaking, and Yu-kuang was panic-stricken. He prostrated himself and wept. He cried, "May the Lords of Heaven be kind and forgive me!"

Ch'ang said, "My friend, you have studied the works of the ancient sages. You value truth in the teachings and you are often inspired by the virtue of others. However, when you close your books and when there is no one to inspire you, you forget your values immediately. Virtue has not taken root in your heart and so your actions are shallow and your motives unclear. Moreover, you do charitable works only as a show for others. Your intentions are impure and your thoughts are devious. How dare you ask for rewards that are given to those who are truly good of heart. You are like the man who sows thorns and thistles and expects a harvest of good fruit. What a fool you are!

"If you want your retribution to lessen, from now on you must be sincere. Be courageous. Drive all evil thoughts from your mind. Fill it with pure and noble thoughts. They will be the foundation for your actions and direct you to good deeds. When a chance to do good arises, do it without hesitation. Do it without considering whether it will be easy or difficult. Do it without thinking of reward or praise. If the task is beyond your strength, do the best you can. Remember, patience is your responsibility, and perseverance is your duty. Above all, avoid indifference and self-deception. When you have followed this advice for a long time, the benefits of your actions will naturally come to you.

"I have given you this advice because within your home you have served me sincerely. If you carry out my instructions immediately you may appease the anger of the Lords of Heaven and redress the wrongs that you have done."

While speaking, the strange old man gradually receded to the far end of the house. Yu-kuang followed eagerly, but as he approached the kitchen hearth, the old man disappeared. Yu-kuang then realized that his visitor was the God of the Hearth, whose duty it was to report a household's good and evil deeds to the Lords of Heaven [see note 4, chapter 3, p.9]. Gratefully, Yu-kuang burned incense and offered his thanks for the god's guidance.

The next day was the first day of the year and Yu-kuang offered his respects to Heaven reverently. From that day on, he avoided his former errors and did everything with a sincere and compassionate heart. He changed his literary name to Cheng-I Tao-jen, which means "the Taoist who is devoted to purifying his heart". Moreover, he wrote an oath in which he pledged to rid himself of all evil thoughts.

At first, Yu found himself faced with conflict and indecision. He slid into self-doubt and indifference. However, he battled against the monsters of his mind courageously and soon returned to the state of mind he had attained before going astray. He prostrated himself before the altar of Kuan-yin in his home and wept, saying, "I vow that my only desire will be to fill my mind with noble and worthy thoughts. I pledge to use all my strength to uphold the values of good."

Every day he rose early and sincerely invoked one hundred times the sacred name of the Boddhisattva of Great Compassion. From that moment he could control his thoughts and actions as if he were being aided by the deities. When he saw a chance to help others, be they human or beast, he offered himself sincerely. He did not consider any task too great or too small nor ask himself whether he had the time or resources or whether his deeds would be known to anyone. He laboured unceasingly until the task at hand was finished. He did charitable works whenever and wherever he could, remaining quiet and unassuming in all he did. He studied the classics as he had never done before. He practised humility, bore insults without holding grudges and tirelessly encouraged others to do the same. The days passed quickly and Yu began to find them too short for all the good works he wished to do. On the last day of every month he listed his actions on a slip of yellow paper and burned it in front of the hearth.

Time went by, and Yu-kuang's actions began to bear fruit. While he was engaged in doing good deeds, his mind did not have time for evil thoughts. As a result, his mind was serene and free from anxiety. This continued for three years.

When Yu-kuang was fifty years old, during the second year of the reign of Wan-li [1574], Ch'ang Kiang-lin, the First Minister of the State, was looking for a tutor for his son. By then, Yu's reputation as a man of virtue was known far and wide. Everyone recommended Yu for the position. The minister personally went to invite Yu into his service and brought him and his family to live in the capital.

The minister was so impressed by Yu's strength of character that he encouraged Yu to take the imperial examinations. Yu completed the examinations with distinction and was awarded the degree of Licentiate. The next year he received the rank of Doctor of Studies.

Yu was now in the company of the emperor's inner circle of officials. One day, he went to visit a eunuch by the name of Yang-kuang. Yang introduced his five adopted sons to Yu-kuang. The eunuch had purchased boys in different parts of the country so that he might have "sons" to comfort him in his old age. As Yu greeted them, he was met by a stare from one of the boys. The face looked very familiar so Yu asked the young man where he was from. The youth replied, "I was born in the district of Kiang-shih. When I was eight I was playing in the street and carelessly climbed on to a wagon. I soon lost my way and could not find my family's house. I have only dim memories of my village and my family."

Yu-kuang was astonished. In great excitement he asked the young man to take off his left shoe. Seeing the two black birthmarks, Yu-kuang exclaimed, "You are my son!" His friend the eunuch was deeply moved by this reunion and allowed the father to take his son home. When Yu-kuang's wife embraced her son, both mother and boy wept with joy. As he pressed his face to hers, the boy's tongue touched his mother's eyes and instantly the mother regained her sight. Yu-kuang was now truly happy. Although his eyes were filled with tears, his face beamed with joy.

Yu-kuang gave up his government post and said goodbye to his benefactor, the minister Ch'ang Kiang-lin. He wished to retire and return to his home town with his family. The minister had grown fond of Yu and loaded him with riches and fine goods before they parted.

Yu-kuang eventually reached his ancestral home. He settled into a happy and contented life, and continued doing good deeds with the same sincerity and diligence as before. His son married and had seven sons. The son and the grandchildren all lived to inherit the renown and talent of Yu-kuang.

In his old age, Yu-kuang wrote a book describing the experiences of his life. He gave it to his grandchildren so that they could learn from his example. He lived to the age of eighty-eight years and everyone saw his happy and long life as a proof that good deeds can change retribution into reward.

The Dragon Lord sends a storm

The Dragon Lord's Wrath

In the town of Tai-shang there lived an extremely wealthy and cruel man named Shen. He was inhumane to his subordinates and inconsiderate to his fellow citizens. Shen also delighted in making life difficult for others by sabotaging their work. He secretly arranged to have farming, hunting and manufacturing equipment damaged so he could revel in the misery of others.

Once, Shen hired a sculptor called Lu to carve figures on beams and pillars in a guest house he was building. When the artist finished the work, Shen refused to pay. Lu took the matter to the local magistrate and the court settled the dispute against Shen. Shen was furious and resolved to get revenge on the sculptor.

Some time later, the Buddhist temple in the city was building a new hall. The priests had heard of Lu's fame as a sculptor and invited him to carve the figures of the Five Hundred Arhats. Shen thought his chance for revenge against Lu had arrived. Secretly, he hired a thug and instructed him to join Lu's party of assistants. On the way to the temple, the villain carried out Shen's bidding by damaging some of the sculptor's tools and absconding with the rest. When Lu arrived at the temple without the appropriate tools he was unable to compete with the rest of the sculptors. As a result, Lu lost the commission and became destitute.

Shen's daughter-in-law did not approve of his evil schemes and told him that unless he reformed, his acts would anger the Lords of Heaven and retribution would come to him and his family. Shen rejected her advice and berated her for being disrespectful and impudent. He drove her out of the house, telling her never to return.

The daughter-in-law had scarcely gone a mile from Shen's mansion when she heard a loud crack of thunder. Lightning split the skies and torrential rain fell. She ran into the woods and hid in a deserted shack. Out of the window, she saw the skies open and a scarlet dragon come out of the rain clouds to descend into Shen's mansion. Instantly all the buildings in the mansion collapsed and everything inside was destroyed.

The only member of Shen's household to survive was his daughter-in-law. The Lords of Heaven favoured her and she lived a long and prosperous life.

TRANSLATOR'S NOTE

The arhats are disciples of the Buddha and are considered guardians of the Dharma (the principles of Buddhism).

Ho-kuan visits the kingdom of the ants

Ho-kuan and the Ants

Ho-kuan of the village Kuang-nan was a kind-hearted man who had never killed a living creature in his life. Ho-kuan was not very wealthy but had a jar containing a thousand silver pieces that were his life's savings. He kept the jar in a wooden chest, but one night termites that had infested the area where he lived bore into the chest and ate part of the silver.

When his family discovered this, they traced the ants to a hollow cave and found a colony of millions of termites. They proposed to destroy the ants, thinking that this might recover some of the lost silver. However, Ho-kuan objected to the plan, saying, "I cannot bear to see many creatures killed on account of a small sum of silver." So his family let the matter drop.

That night Ho had a dream. He saw many soldiers in white armour coming towards him, inviting him to their palace to see their king. Ho boarded their carriage and was taken to a magnificent and prosperous city. Numerous dignitaries met him at the gate of the palace and escorted him in. The king rose when he saw Ho and descended from the throne to meet him. He greeted Ho and said, "Through your benevolence we have been saved from our enemy. However, we have inconvenienced you in the process. Due to your kindness, my subjects have escaped a great calamity. I cannot thank you enough for what you have done for my kingdom. There is a small tree near your home. Beneath the tree is a jar of silver that was buried during ancient times. Dig it up and keep the treasure as a token of our thanks. You represent all that is good in humanity. It's a pity that you are too old to enjoy the fruits of your kindness yourself. However, your descendants will benefit from what you have sown."

After his audience with the king, Ho-kuan was escorted back to his own house by the white-armoured soldiers. When he awoke from his dream, he realized that it was the ants who had come to him. He found the tree the ant-king described, dug underneath it, and retrieved a jar of silver. His descendants enjoyed the prosperity brought by this treasure for many generations.

The cruel hunters shoot at the deer spirit

The Cruel Hunters

In the county of Hsiang-tan in Hu-kuang district there lived an old gentleman who was much respected by the community. However, he had three sons who did not care for culture or learning. They preferred hunting to studying, and spent much of their time roaming in the mountains in search of game.

One day the three youths went hunting with a large party of young people and met an old man in a white robe. The man knelt before them and said, "Refrain from killing and awaken to the nature of goodness in you. The respect for life practised by the sages is a universal value. It is now spring. This is a time when nature renews itself and everything grows again. If you do not possess the compassion and tenderness of the sages, your wild emotions and rash actions will destroy many living things. If you wantonly kill animals or set the woods on fire, you will incur the wrath of the Lords of Heaven. I am a poor creature who has seven young children. There is not enough time to move them to a place of safety. Please spare us and we will remember your kindness forever."

The three leaders of the party of hunters did not fully understand what the strange old man said, but without further thought they promised to do what he requested.

When the old man had left, the hunting party began to wonder who he was. Some said his manner of speech did not sound human. Others suggested he might be the spirit of an old animal living in the wilds. The party decided to find out more about this strange creature and set off after him. They caught sight of the old man as he went into a cave. Hoping to drive out whatever was inside, they spread a net and lit a fire at the cave entrance.

Suddenly, a white stag darted from the cave, broke through the net and climbed on to the rocky ledge above. The stag changed into the figure of the old man who turned to the hunters, saying, "You have killed my seven daughters and you shall pay for this cruel act. A disaster ten times the one I have suffered will come to your family."

The three young men tried to shoot the old man, but he caught all their arrows in his hands, broke them into pieces and disappeared.

Not long after this incident, a Taoist monk arrived at the house of the three young men and predicted they would have an imperial future and great prosperity. Excited by the monk's oracle, the young men organized a rebellion and induced their friends to join them. While preparations for the uprising were being made, someone betrayed them to the government. The local authorities immediately sent soldiers to surround the house and had everyone in the family arrested. On examination they were found guilty of treason. Seventy members, relations and associates of the family were executed and the entire clan was wiped out. As for the Taoist monk and the man who betrayed the three young men, nothing was ever heard from them again.

TRANSLATOR'S NOTE

The ability of animals to adopt human form is a popular theme in Chinese folklore. Certain places in nature are thought to contain unusual concentrations of earth energy. If an animal absorbs the primordial energy of the earth, it can shed its animal form. The stronger the energy, the longer the animal can remain in human form. Animals who are capable of taking on human form are considered as almost "immortal" in the animal world and are said to possess magical qualities. It appears that some animals are inherently more disposed to acquire energy and adopt human form. Among these animals are deer, snakes, foxes and monkeys.

Master Moy Lin-shin

Fung Loy Kok Institute
of Taoism

Fung Loy Kok Institute of Taoism is a charitable organization dedicated to promoting Chinese culture and the Taoist arts. Taoist training involves cultivating a mind of compassion and cultivating a body of perfect health. Fung Loy Kok teaches self-cultivation through Taoist arts such as chanting, meditation, chi-kung, scriptural study and internal exercises, and promotes charity through community service. The programmes and activities of the Institute's centres and its affiliated organizations, the Taoist Tai Chi Society and the Gei Pang Lok Hup Academy, are open to all.

Fung Loy Kok, which means "Islands of the Immortal Realm", traces its lineage through the Earlier Heaven Wu-chi sect, founded by the Patriarch Tien-lung who received the teachings of the Tao from Chen Hsi-I, fifth Patriarch of Huashan. For centuries, the teachings were transmitted to enlightened teachers within the Taoist monastic community in China. The widespread war and suffering which greeted the arrival of the twentieth century in China convinced Taoist teachers that the transmission should no longer be restricted to the monasteries.

Master Moy Lin-shin, a monk who studied the Taoist arts of health and longevity for over thirty years in China and Hong Kong, emigrated to Canada in 1970 and founded the Taoist T'ai Chi Society in that year. In 1981, he established Fung Loy Kok and, in 1988, the Gei Pang Lok Hup Academy. These three organisations co-ordinate their efforts to preserve and foster the continued development of Taoist philosophy, arts and rituals, and have opened centres in many countries.

The Translation Committee of Fung Loy Kok Institute of Taoism was formed to make the writings of Taoism available to the non-Chinese-reading public. The committee consists of Institute members who volunteer their expertise and time in preparing translations of the Taoist canon, original works of interpretation, and commentary on Taoist texts.

The translator, Dr. Eva Wong, is currently the Director of Studies at the Fung Loy Kok Institute of Taoism and a member of the State of Colorado's Interfaith Advisory Council of the Governor. She also offers graduate-level courses on Taoist and Buddhist Philosophy at the University of Denver. Her books, *Seven Taoist Masters* and *Cultivating Stillness*, are published by Shambhala Publications.

Centres of the Fung Loy Kok Institute of Taoism

Sam Dip Tem, Tsuen Wan, New Territories, Hong Kong

49 West 11th Avenue, Denver, Colorado 80204, USA

1310 North Monroe Street, Tallahassee, Florida 32303, USA

1376 Bathurst Street, Toronto, Ontario M5R 3J1, Canada

134 D'Arcy Street, Toronto, Ontario M5T 1R3, Canada

2310 24th Street SW, Calgary, Alberta T2T 0G6, Canada

15740 Stony Plain Road, Edmonton, Alberta T5P 3Z5, Canada

12 Cooper Street, First Floor, Surrey Hills, Sydney, New South Wales 2120, Australia